*Energy Accounting*

T0385196

# Energy
# Accounting

### Stress Management and Mental Health Monitoring for Autism and Related Conditions

## Maja Toudal
## and Tony Attwood

**Jessica Kingsley Publishers**
London and Philadelphia

First published in Great Britain in 2025 by Jessica Kingsley Publishers
An imprint of John Murray Press

2

The information contained in this book is not intended to replace the services
of trained medical professionals or to be a substitute for medical advice. You
are advised to consult a doctor on any matters relating to your health, and in
particular on any matters that may require diagnosis or medical attention.

A CIP catalogue record for this title is available from the
British Library and the Library of Congress

ISBN 978 1 78775 775 2
eISBN 978 1 78775 774 5

Printed and bound in the UK by Ashford Colour Ltd.

Jessica Kingsley Publishers' policy is to use papers that are natural,
renewable and recyclable products and made from wood grown in sus-
tainable forests. The logging and manufacturing processes are expected
to conform to the environmental regulations of the country of origin.

Jessica Kingsley Publishers
Carmelite House
50 Victoria Embankment
London EC4Y 0DZ

www.jkp.com

John Murray Press
Part of Hodder & Stoughton Ltd
An Hachette Company

The authorised representative in the EEA is Hachette Ireland, 8 Castlecourt Centre,
Castleknock Road, Castleknock, Dublin 15, D15 YF6A, Ireland

# Contents

## PART 3: STAGES OF ENERGY ACCOUNTING

## PART 4: MAKING ADJUSTMENTS

## PART 5: CLINICAL IMPLEMENTATION

# Acknowledgements

## Maja Toudal

Very few books in this world come into existence without being influenced by a number of people along the way. With regard to this one, a great number of people have helped to inspire and shape the contents, each in their own way.

It should come as no surprise that Energy Accounting, as a general idea, is neither new nor unique. Many forms of it exist, and many people have adapted each form to suit their own personal needs or way of thinking. I have been working on my version of Energy Accounting for 15 or more years, and have been inspired by a great many people and ideas. Indeed, many people have either taught me, or directed me towards the knowledge that has laid the foundation for much of the contents of this book.

As such, a number of people should be credited with introducing me to the elements that have combined to create my version of Energy Accounting, and I dearly hope I have remembered them all. Danish autism expert and psychologist Kirsten Callesen was instrumental in my journey of self-reflection and understanding. She continues to be at the forefront of gathering new knowledge and teaching everyone around her, and I greatly admire and appreciate the work she does. The Danish psychologist Trine Uhrskov and Danish autism consultant Christina Sommer were also a part of my learning about stress management. Nana Lykkebo, a fellow autistic person, was, I believe, the first to introduce the concept of colour coding to me albeit in a different form.

In some way, each of my teachers, good and bad, contributed to this book, along with the entire school system in Denmark, because without the intense need to find strategies to survive school, I would never have created Energy Accounting. There have been many versions of this book, and many people have read and contributed feedback in their own way. Without them, this book would be very different and, might I say, not nearly as good. Thank you all for the time you spent and all the comments and suggestions you took the time to write.

Thank you especially to my friend Haddy, who has helped so much with crafting ideas for the illustrations – since I cannot draw to save my life.

Thank you to my guildmates from World of Warcraft, who encouraged me when I felt as if the task was too vast, and several of whom also took the time to read drafts, each from their own perspective as psychologists, teachers and parents.

Thank you to my family, who showed tremendous patience when I complained that this book would never be finished, and calmly encouraged me not only to keep at it, but also to take my own advice and take breaks, not expect too much of myself (especially as I was attempting to write this book while I studied at university) and make sure I was taking care of myself during the whole process.

To my husband, who did all of this and more, and who has been my greatest supporter over the last 19 years, there is so much more than this book that would never have happened without you, and I am so grateful to have someone who believes in me as much as you do.

Lastly, thank you dearly to Tony, who somehow, magically, decided many years ago that he was willing to write this book with me.

Thank you for putting up with my many ideas and my aspirations, and for encouraging me always.

## *Tony Attwood*

I would like to acknowledge the contributions of my clients to the development of Energy Accounting. We have explored so many energy withdrawals and deposits, a process that has been illuminating and practical in terms of improving well-being, mental health and a sense of self.

Thank you to my colleagues who have expressed their appreciation of Energy Accounting as a valuable clinical tool that they intuitively know will improve their ability to understand and support their clients. They have so often asked, 'When is the book going to be published?'

I also acknowledge my own support team in terms of family and colleagues, who have recognized that Energy Accounting has become my passion.

# Preface

Energy Accounting has broad applications and can be used by anyone who wishes to work towards improving their stress management skills and quality of life. The two authors of this book work primarily in the field of autism and, for this reason, many examples will include this perspective. This means there are numerous mentions of autism, autistic people and autistic experiences.

The term autism describes someone who has different abilities and challenges in their daily life. There are specific diagnostic criteria for autism spectrum disorder (ASD) that have been refined over several decades and are used by clinicians and academics. However, there has recently been considerable discussion and different perspectives put forward on whether autism describes a mental disorder within the province of psychiatry or a valued part of human neurodiversity. There have been changes in terminology, led by autistic individuals, that are beginning to be accepted by academics and clinicians, as well as the broader community rather than only autistic people themselves. The term autism spectrum disorder is increasingly being replaced with *autism spectrum condition* (ASC) and there is a growing preference for identity-first language, such as the term *autistic person* rather than *person with autism*. In this book, we use identity-first language as preferred by the autistic community, and the term autism in reference to a neurotype rather than a diagnostic label.

Energy Accounting is based on our combined clinical and personal experience. We anticipate that there will eventually be research on the effectiveness of Energy Accounting so that it is established as an evidence-based intervention. At present, the value of Energy Accounting is based on clinical experience rather than research data.

## HOW TO USE THIS BOOK

Energy Accounting was created to help autistic individuals, those in their support network, and professionals specializing in autism. The descriptions of energy withdrawal and deposit will provide insight into fluctuating energy levels and mood, and the accounting process suggests strategies to reduce stress and increase a sense of well-being.

The book is both a self-help manual and a workbook that can be incorporated into a therapy programme. We recommend reading the entire book to determine how the individual can best benefit from Energy Accounting, then commencing stage 1 and subsequent stages at a pace based on capacity and circumstances.

At various points throughout the book, readers are directed to additional online resources that will help in the application of Energy Accounting. These can be accessed and downloaded by visiting www.jkp.com/catalogue/book/9781787757752

# PART 1

# INTRODUCTIONS TO KEY TOPICS

# Two Case Examples

Here we offer two worked case examples of Energy Accounting in action: one from a 15-year-old autistic adolescent girl and one from a 42-year-old autistic person.

## FIFTEEN-YEAR-OLD AUTISTIC ADOLESCENT GIRL

She was referred for concern regarding episodic depression, high stress levels and meltdowns at home. With the autistic adolescent and her mother, we first explored her energy withdrawals and made a list of situations that drain her mental energy. We then focused on a form of 'currency', which is a numerical measure or value of how much an activity or experience is energy draining for her from day to day. We used a currency range of 0–100, with 100 being extreme energy depletion. Each situation will have a range of energy depletion; for example, on some days, socializing with peers at school could drain her to an energy value of only 20 but on other days it could be 100. The entry in the energy account ledger below would be 20–100.

We discovered and discussed situations that were energy draining, such as coping with a surprise test (60–90), but there were several situations that had a much greater energy withdrawal than her mother or the psychologist anticipated. These included being late for class (10–40) as she was greatly stressed by the other students turning to stare at her when she entered the classroom. Another situation that was considerably energy depleting was when her mother became agitated at home (30–100). Her mother's mood was often due to her being annoyed with the adolescent girl's autistic brother and had nothing to do with her. However, her mother's agitation was 'contagious' to her and she consumed considerable mental energy trying not to become agitated herself.

A cause of energy depletion that we predicted was when friends were not nice to each other, as she would spend some time during breaks trying to restore the friendship disagreements between her peers, acting as an arbitrator (20–30). What we had not anticipated was how her friends' disclosure of their personal problems would affect her (20–90). We started to recognize how the well-being and emotional state of others affected her energy levels.

There was also energy depletion from coping with sensory sensitivity, and a change in expectations, such as having a relief teacher and group activities in class (30–40).

The next stage was to explore her sources of energy and the range of currency. A powerful energizer for her was engaging in her special interest, which was reading Harry Potter books (30–80). She found that being with girls was energy draining but being with boys was energy infusing (10–30). Boys were far less emotional than her female peers and she understood and enjoyed their sense of humour. Dancing freestyle in her bedroom after school was a major source of restoring mental energy (30–50). Drawing was another source of mental energy (20–40) and it was important to pass on to her teachers that drawing while she was listening to her teacher in class was not distracting or disrespectful, but an effective means of feeling less stressed and improving focus and concentration.

The range of energy withdrawals and deposits was written on an energy account ledger (below) and a subsequent ledger was completed over a specified time, such as the previous day, week or month. There was one number rather than a range and the totals in the two columns could be calculated. This procedure was designed to determine if the energy account was 'balanced' – that is, had equivalent levels of energy deposits and withdrawals. This was often not the case, and she would become increasingly energy depleted and stressed and would 'sink' into a depression. We had to ensure that she had opportunities to refresh her energy levels, such as spending time reading her Harry Potter books, which were written into her daily diary and encouraged by her parents, and not removed as a form of punishment. We also explained to her teachers about the extra support she needed at school, especially when engaged in group activities with other girls, and in helping her to be less affected by other people's moods by creating a 'mental shield' or 'armour' when other people were upset.

*Energy Account*

| Withdrawals | | Deposits | |
|---|---|---|---|
| Activity/Experience | (0–100) | Activity/Experience | (0–100) |
| Socializing with peers | 20–100 | Reading Harry Potter books | 30–80 |
| Surprise test | 60–90 | Dancing freestyle in bedroom | 30–50 |
| Crowds | 20–60 | Talking to boys at school | 10–30 |
| Mum being cranky | 30–100 | Headphones and music | 20–40 |
| Friends not being nice to each other | 20–30 | Walking | 0–10 |
| Friends' own problems | 20–90 | Drawing in class to focus | 20–40 |
| Noise in class | 20–30 | | |
| Teachers being 'snappy' | 30–50 | | |
| Pre-menstrual tension | 10–30 | | |
| Relief teachers | 20–60 | | |
| Group work | 30–40 | | |

## FORTY-TWO-YEAR-OLD AUTISTIC PERSON

This autistic adult asked for consultation with regard to Energy Accounting, specifically focusing on frequent depressive episodes, and noted from the beginning that sensory and cognitive over-stimulation as well as anxiety seemed to lead to their symptoms getting worse. They had been in therapy before and had a good understanding of themselves in many ways, and many coping mechanisms which generally were useful and effective.

We began by exploring deposits and withdrawals, assigning a value range to each. We made an effort to include as many deposits as we could, as well as different 'categories' of activities and experiences.

*Energy Account*

| Withdrawals | | Deposits | |
|---|---|---|---|
| Activity/Experience | (0–100) | Activity/Experience | (0–100) |
| Reminders of disability/ difference | 20–40 | Stimming | 20–60 |
| Sensory sensitivity triggers, loud noises or flickering lights | 80–100 | Arts/crafts | 10–50 |
| Anxiety/worries | 20–80 | Being with animals | 10–60 |
| Seeing people/socializing Socializing with other autistic people | 20–50 10–40 | Naps/lying with a thick blanket | 20–30 |
| Seeing/meeting new people | 50–90 | Noise-cancelling headphones | 30–70 |
| Pressure (feeling of or real) Having to go somewhere | 30–80 20–40 | Gardening | 30–50 |
| Appointments | 20–40 | Collecting, such as finding fossils or crystals in nature | 30–40 |
| PTSD triggers | 90–100 | Walks | 20–30 |
| People being angry | 70–100 | Thunderstorms | 50–70 |
| Masking | 20–80 | Music | 10–60 |
| | | Games (only works sometimes) | 0–30 |
| | | Museums | 20–40 |
| | | Reading | 20–40 |

Once we had a fair beginning to a list of deposits and withdrawals

– these can always be expanded in more nuance and detail – we continued with a list of stress/depression symptoms, and a list of well-being symptoms. These lists were to be used for self-monitoring purposes, such that the person themselves could notice sooner when their mental health declined. However, self-monitoring also meant that the person could note when the different symptoms appeared, providing data that could be used in the case going forward.

| Stress/depression symptoms | Well-being symptoms |
| --- | --- |
| Social withdrawal | Social interaction is okay |
| Intrusive thoughts | Doing art/crafting for longer at a time |
| Suicidal thoughts | Speech mannerisms are present |
| Loss of appetite and forgetting to eat | Taking bike instead of public transportation |
| Insomnia | Stimming more freely |
| Emotions disappear, except for sadness and hopelessness | Laughing and smiling at the 'little things' |
| Flat, slower speech, loss of speech mannerisms | Singing and dancing feel natural |
| No energy for tidying and cleaning, things become messy | Going for walks in new places, finding pretty places or things |
| Washing hair less often – does not want to leave the room | Being more organized |
| Frequent headaches | Cooking for pleasure rather than survival |
| Usual deposits decrease in value or stop working as strategies (anhedonia) | |

Our next perspective was to look at what times of year we could say with relative certainty would be good or worse with regard to their mental health. This person's home location was unfortunately tied to previous traumatic experiences, and while they were seeking trauma treatment, they had not been able to begin yet. This meant there were constant triggers around.

However, once a year, during August, they travelled with family to a different location, a vacation home, which did not hold traumatic memories for them. For this reason, August was usually a very good mental health period.

After they came home, the reality would set in that it would be a long time before they came back to the vacation home, and therefore also away from the triggers relating to traumatic experiences. This created negative thoughts about being stuck around triggers, missing the good environment they had just been in, and that it would be a very long time before they could go back. These thoughts could be one factor in a downward spiral which led to a depressive episode. We marked this period of time where they were especially sensitive to a depressive episode on a year calendar to serve as a reminder that they must be extra mindful of their mental health during this time.

March and April was another sensitive period, because it was a very long time since they had had a break from their daily environment. This meant they had been essentially in 'survival mode' for too long, and the constant triggers of traumatic experiences made it very difficult to keep their energy account balanced. This period was also marked.

The gaps not marked by sensitive periods were usually better due to knowing the dates of the next trip. The promise that it would happen helped them hold themselves together.

With all these points of data gathered, we could begin to test changes, and see if perhaps we could alleviate the negative thoughts and mental exhaustion.

Initial suggestions to try out included:

- Planned weekends at their parents' house. This place was not connected with traumatic experiences, and although they could not live there full time, they could still go to stay for a few days sometimes.

| JANUARY | | FEBRUARY | | MARCH | | APRIL | | MAY | | JUNE | |
|---|---|---|---|---|---|---|---|---|---|---|---|
| 1 | | 1 | | 1 | | 1 | | 1 | | 1 | |
| 2 | | 2 | | 2 | | 2 | | 2 | | 2 | |
| 3 | | 3 | | 3 | | 3 | | 3 | | 3 | |
| 4 | | 4 | | 4 | | 4 | | 4 | | 4 | |
| 5 | | 5 | | 5 | | 5 | | 5 | | 5 | |
| 6 | | 6 | | 6 | | 6 | | 6 | | 6 | |
| 7 | | 7 | | 7 | | 7 | SENSITIVE TO | 7 | | 7 | |
| 8 | | 8 | | 8 | | 8 | DEPRESSIVE | 8 | | 8 | |
| 9 | | 9 | | 9 | | 9 | EPISODE | 9 | | 9 | |
| 10 | | 10 | | 10 | | 10 | | 10 | | 10 | |
| 11 | | 11 | | 11 | | 11 | | 11 | | 11 | |
| 12 | | 12 | | 12 | | 12 | | 12 | | 12 | |
| 13 | | 13 | | 13 | | 13 | | 13 | | 13 | |
| 14 | | 14 | | 14 | | 14 | | 14 | (POSSIBLE) | 14 | |
| 15 | | 15 | | 15 | | 15 | | 15 | VACATION | 15 | |
| 16 | | 16 | | 16 | | 16 | | 16 | BREAK | 16 | |
| 17 | | 17 | | 17 | | 17 | | 17 | | 17 | |
| 18 | | 18 | | 18 | | 18 | | 18 | | 18 | |
| 19 | | 19 | | 19 | | 19 | | 19 | | 19 | |
| 20 | | 20 | | 20 | | 20 | | 20 | | 20 | |
| 21 | | 21 | | 21 | | 21 | | 21 | | 21 | |
| 22 | | 22 | | 22 | | 22 | | 22 | | 22 | |
| 23 | | 23 | | 23 | | 23 | | 23 | | 23 | |
| 24 | | 24 | | 24 | | 24 | | 24 | | 24 | |
| 25 | | 25 | | 25 | SENSITIVE TO | 25 | | 25 | | 25 | |
| 26 | | 26 | | 26 | DEPRESSIVE | 26 | | 26 | | 26 | |
| 27 | | 27 | | 27 | EPISODE | 27 | | 27 | | 27 | |
| 28 | | 28 | | 28 | | 28 | | 28 | | 28 | |
| 29 | | | | 29 | | 29 | | 29 | | 29 | |
| 30 | | | | 30 | | 30 | | 30 | | 30 | |
| 31 | | | | 31 | | | | 31 | | | |

| JULY | | AUGUST | | SEPTEMBER | | OCTOBER | | NOVEMBER | | DECEMBER | |
|---|---|---|---|---|---|---|---|---|---|---|---|
| 1 | | 1 | | 1 | | 1 | | 1 | | 1 | |
| 2 | | 2 | | 2 | | 2 | | 2 | | 2 | |
| 3 | | 3 | | 3 | | 3 | | 3 | | 3 | |
| 4 | | 4 | | 4 | | 4 | | 4 | | 4 | |
| 5 | | 5 | | 5 | | 5 | | 5 | | 5 | |
| 6 | | 6 | | 6 | | 6 | | 6 | | 6 | |
| 7 | | 7 | | 7 | | 7 | | 7 | | 7 | |
| 8 | | 8 | | 8 | | 8 | | 8 | SENSITIVE TO | 8 | |
| 9 | | 9 | | 9 | | 9 | | 9 | DEPRESSIVE | 9 | |
| 10 | | 10 | | 10 | | 10 | | 10 | EPISODE | 10 | |
| 11 | | 11 | | 11 | | 11 | | 11 | | 11 | |
| 12 | | 12 | | 12 | | 12 | | 12 | | 12 | |
| 13 | | 13 | | 13 | | 13 | | 13 | | 13 | |
| 14 | | 14 | VACATION | 14 | | 14 | | 14 | | 14 | |
| 15 | | 15 | BREAK | 15 | | 15 | | 15 | | 15 | |
| 16 | | 16 | | 16 | | 16 | | 16 | | 16 | |
| 17 | | 17 | | 17 | | 17 | | 17 | | 17 | |
| 18 | | 18 | | 18 | | 18 | | 18 | | 18 | |
| 19 | | 19 | | 19 | | 19 | | 19 | | 19 | |
| 20 | | 20 | | 20 | | 20 | | 20 | | 20 | |
| 21 | | 21 | | 21 | | 21 | | 21 | | 21 | |
| 22 | | 22 | | 22 | | 22 | SENSITIVE TO | 22 | | 22 | |
| 23 | | 23 | | 23 | | 23 | DEPRESSIVE | 23 | | 23 | |
| 24 | | 24 | | 24 | | 24 | EPISODE | 24 | | 24 | |
| 25 | | 25 | | 25 | | 25 | | 25 | | 25 | |
| 26 | | 26 | | 26 | | 26 | | 26 | | 26 | |
| 27 | | 27 | | 27 | | 27 | | 27 | | 27 | |
| 28 | | 28 | | 28 | | 28 | | 28 | | 28 | |
| 29 | | 29 | | 29 | | 29 | | 29 | | 29 | |
| 30 | | 30 | | 30 | | 30 | | 30 | | 30 | |
| 31 | | 31 | | | | 31 | | | | 31 | |

- One big outing, for example a museum or a music show, during each sensitive period. These outings would need to be planned well in advance. This would add financial stress, but would also be something to look forward to. Their parents could help with the finances sometimes, and otherwise they would be there to offer emotional support.
- Taking a short break from appointments, for example two weeks, but with the caveat that if their mental health declined rather than improved, they would contact their support people even if it was a 'no appointment' period. Removing appointments would be risky as it would remove support in some ways, but it would also take away big reminders of their disability, which was a constant stressor and greatly affected their sense of self-esteem.
- Outsourcing phone calls and dealing with mail. These were anxiety triggers all year round, but for the sensitive periods, someone else could take care of them, to remove as much of the stress as possible. Family members and friends could help with this, although with the agreement that they may have to ask questions about how to deal with certain things.

It was important to monitor the person's well-being regularly, and make changes as needed. Changes which made a greater difference were prioritized, and those which made less of an impact were seen as more optional. If any changes were discovered to make no difference or have a negative impact, they were scrapped; however, some changes did not show their worth for several months.

Over the following year, we saw that the greatest difference appeared to come from planning weekends at their parents' house, and getting away from their own home. Naturally, any options for moving permanently were continuously explored, as was any progress in obtaining and going through trauma therapy.

- **SEE RESOURCE 1**: *An Introduction to Autism Spectrum Disorder.*

# CHAPTER 1

# *What is Energy Accounting?*

The Energy Accounting process presented in this book is a stress management method that combines a number of elements from existing stress management techniques with aspects from our experience that we have found useful and meaningful in our personal and professional lives. This approach allows for greater personalization, applicability and flexibility, and includes a range of tools which are designed to improve stress management, quality of life and achievements. Importantly, Energy Accounting is an adaptable method which enables each person to tailor the elements to suit their own situation.

Energy Accounting also takes current clinical and academic knowledge of autism into account; however, Energy Accounting can be useful for any person who wants a way to manage stress in their life. In other words, the Energy Accounting method is not autism-specific, but it is created and presented with autistic people in mind.

● **SEE RESOURCE 2:** *A Personal Perspective.*

## EXPECTATIONS AND ADVICE FOR THE APPLICATION OF ENERGY ACCOUNTING

When any psychological method or therapeutic approach is proposed, there will be questions regarding its use, as well as its results. In this section, we provide advice to address any questions we expect a reader may want answered sooner rather than later.

## Use Energy Accounting as a complementary therapy to existing treatment

People who find themselves wanting to manage stress and refocus on their quality of life are quite likely to have gone through, or be going through, a period of their lives which is marked by stressors, symptoms of depression, anxiety or perhaps other mental health challenges. We suggest that any existing treatment, whether that be other forms of therapy or medication, remains in place.

Energy Accounting can be used effectively as a complementary therapy, approaching the person's challenges from a new angle. For example, Energy Accounting has been used as a part of an effective treatment programme for depression in autistic teenagers and young adults (Attwood & Garnett 2016). It should never *replace* the direct treatment of a psychiatric illness, disorder or condition, but it can serve to aid the person in re-examining their energy depletion and restoration, and how these factor into their daily lives. Consider Energy Accounting as a set of additional tools in an already existing strategy toolbox or library for helping an individual to accommodate their needs in managing stress and enhancing their quality of life (Attwood & Garnett 2016).

## Energy Accounting should be personalized

As is done with many other forms of treatment, even psychopharmacological treatments, Energy Accounting should be moulded to fit the person's needs, rather than attempting to make the individual fit into the 'box'. We will be reminding the reader of this point throughout the book.

Personalizing a therapeutic method is important for several reasons. Every person has different needs – they may not require every element of Energy Accounting. There is simply no need to waste time on elements that do not seem to have any use for that person. Also, every person has different preferences – and we find that, clinically, methods and approaches only tend to be helpful if they appeal to the person. This means that if someone finds colour coding to be cumbersome or perhaps juvenile, then it will only become an annoyance to them rather than an aid. For this reason, the Energy Accounting laid out in this book should serve as a template from which you can continuously customize according to individual needs.

*Have patience, especially when you want to hurry*
When first learning about Energy Accounting, it can be tempting to implement it all very quickly. However, Energy Accounting was created such that we can take smaller steps and become familiar with each one before adding another. In fact, this is the recommended way to use Energy Accounting. As you will see in our clinical programme outline later in the book, each element of Energy Accounting can be added separately and can be used to explore the person's needs and further develop their self-understanding. This is best done if not rushed, as rushing through the exploration of elements of Energy Accounting will often result in less emphasis on reflection, fewer details, as well as not being fully comfortable with each element before adding another.

Another reason to explore and implement the approach more slowly is that people often need more processing time than they are immediately aware of, especially if they are very stressed or have been suffering from depression or anxiety for a prolonged period. Autistic people often need a bit of time to adjust to new ideas, even if the presentation is designed to be 'autism friendly', either due to extended cognitive processing time or to the preference for sameness and aversion to change that many autistic people have.

This being said, some people do process new information very quickly or have little patience for details once they have understood the overarching ideas. This is okay, of course, and for such people, we recommend that a faster introduction to elements can occur, with the intention to revisit each element as it becomes relevant for the therapeutic programme for that individual.

# CHAPTER 2

## What is Stress?

The word stress is used all the time in daily life. In daily speech, stress is something we feel, something we are, or it is an external enemy, an illness, to be fought off. When we work with stress, however, we view stress in the sense of strain or overload.

Strain and overload are connected to the idea of attempting to meet demands that exceed your resources, leading eventually to symptoms such as feeling unusually tired/fatigued, drained and sometimes irritable. It is quite normal for those who experience longer-term stress to feel guilt and shame, and to develop a more negative sense of self. An overview of some common symptoms of stress can be found later in this chapter.

Burnout refers to a kind of stress where a long period of overload leads to the person 'breaking' in a sense. Everyday tasks seem completely insurmountable, there can be physical symptoms such as vomiting, visual disturbances, problems with movement, and much else. Often there are sleep disturbances in one form or another.

The following sections will explore stress and burnout in greater depth. We will explain some of the biological mechanisms as well as the consequences of stress, and common symptoms, and provide a general introduction to current thinking on stress. A section on treatment and recovery can be found in the downloadable material. The biology of stress is quite complicated, and, for that reason, this will be a somewhat short and simplified explanation.

## STRESS RESPONSES

A stress response is not the same as stress or burnout, but it can be helpful to many people to understand the physiology of stress responses when talking about stress and burnout on a symptomatic or behavioural level. As such, a simplified explanation of physiological stress responses can provide a mental framework for thinking about one's reactions in daily life.

Stress responses happen when we are confronted with perceived threats. This includes obvious things like a dangerous animal, fire or natural disasters. It also includes social threats, and other threats to our well-being, such as situations like our work or school environment making demands that we feel unable to meet, verbal attacks being made towards us or people we care about, or being confronted with a new type of problem that we do not know how to solve. There are four main factors that elicit stress responses:

1. Novelty.
2. Unpredictability.
3. A decreased sense of control.
4. A threat to one's ego.

That last one may lead people to think that it applies to people who feel proud or who are egocentric in some way. However, threats to your ego or sense of self can include experiences such as being bullied, facing discrimination, failing at a task that you perceive as easy, or having to give a speech or perform an ability in front of people who are evaluating you.

When a stress response happens, the so-called stress axes are activated and you experience some form of a fight, flight, freeze or fawn response. These responses are what we can observe in people's behaviour, but behind the scenes – inside our bodies – there is a lot going on.

## The fight, flight, freeze and fawn responses

Many people have probably heard to some degree of the fight or flight response. When animals (including us) are faced with a threat, the two most obvious responses, and perhaps the most common, are to either fight the threat or to run away – hence fight or flight. In humans, we see both of these responses as well, with some people being more likely to fight or to flee.

However, some animals freeze instead. In some cases, this is true for the species as a whole, opossums being a specific example. In other cases, it is a response that is sometimes observed, but not always, and this is true for humans too.

When faced with a threat, sometimes people are unable to act or choose, and seem to become mentally and/or physically paralysed. They cannot scream, run or find a solution, and instead become 'frozen in fear'.

A more recent documented response, and one we are still learning to understand, is the fawn response. Fawning refers to a type of behaviour that seems to accommo-date the attacker, and is done in order to survive. It is a people-pleasing type of behaviour that is often seen in people with complex trauma, such as survivors of abusive relationships, but that also occurs in single events. Some sexual assault survivors, for example, describe attempting to appease their attacker during the attack, in an effort to survive. It can involve agreeing to things they do not want to, setting aside personal feelings and even boundaries or values.

The fawn response is every bit as involuntary as the others, and, just like the others, can take a long time to unlearn or regulate.

There are a number of hormones and neurotransmitters that moderate or are involved in stress responses. Here, we begin by focusing on just two: one is very well known in everyday language – adrenaline; the other, slightly less well known, is cortisol.

Adrenaline and cortisol both serve useful functions in our bodies. In low doses or when we are exposed to them for a relatively short time, these hormones work by allowing us to adapt to threats, act when we need to and then calm back down. However, when we are exposed to very high levels or we are over-exposed for long periods of time, problems such as severe or prolonged stress symptoms or psychiatric issues such as anxiety or post-traumatic stress disorder (PTSD) arise. We can say that biological stress becomes toxic to our internal systems – our brains, nervous system, our whole body.

Again, not everyone reacts in the same way to things, and what is stressful to one person is not to another, and what is very stressful for one may only be mildly stressful for another. We are all different, and how we think and feel about these threats can have a major impact on the biological response (and vice versa).

Adrenaline and cortisol are released when the stress axes are activated. These are called the sympatho-adrenomedullary (SAM) axis and the hypothalamic-pituitary-adrenal (HPA) axis. A brief and simplified explanation – which is sufficient for our needs right now – is that the SAM axis is the adrenal system and is quick and short-acting, while the HPA axis is the slower and longer-acting cortisol system. In a threatening situation, both axes are activated. However, they serve different functions.

The adrenal system spurs us to action, meaning that this is largely what controls or mediates the fight or flight response. Meanwhile, the cortisol system is what helps our bodies to adapt to repeated or long-term stress exposure. You could say that it teaches our bodies how to react next time.

When the threat is gone, the SAM and HPA axes are designed to shut down, meaning they stop producing adrenaline and cortisol. They have done their job, reacted to the threat, and now they can calm down, have a rest and be ready for whenever we need them again. The axes shutting down allows the body to exit survival mode. This process is called feedback inhibition. It is a strange scientific term, but it could be translated as: the feedback loop which makes the stress systems activate and stay activated is slowed down and stopped, like applying the brakes to a moving vehicle. Our systems are inhibiting the feedback that makes the adrenaline and cortisol keep pumping. This is good. We want this to happen, because otherwise we would constantly be in survival mode, ready to face down a threat that is not there. We do not fully understand how feedback inhibition happens, but evidence suggests that serotonin and oxytocin hormones play a role in regulating stress reactivity and the feedback inhibition of the HPA axis.

## TOLERABLE AND TOXIC STRESS

Importantly, this whole process – that the perception of some kind of threat leads to a stress response which involves adrenaline and cortisol, and that these stress hormones stop being produced when the threat is over – is a crucial part of how humans (and all other animals with these stress systems) have survived.

We differentiate between three 'types' of stress: good stress, tolerable stress and toxic stress. Good stress is what happens when we take a chance or risk and feel rewarded when we are successful, such as completing and doing well at an exam, interview or public speaking. These are events that often make us feel nervous, but when that nervousness is manageable and we overcome it, that is an example of good stress.

Tolerable stress is when something bad happens, such as a death in the family, job loss or a divorce, but we have the personal capacity as well as the support systems we need to cope. Tolerable stress is unpleasant and sometimes drawn out, but what makes it tolerable is the ability to 'keep our heads above water'.

Toxic stress is what happens when we do not have the resources or support we need, and our mental and physical health suffers over time.

So why does this happen? Why do we experience clinical (toxic) stress and burnout? In short, when a stressor is too intense, or the physiological stress response is activated too often over a period of time, feedback inhibition can stop working properly. This means our bodies cannot shut down the stress axes, and cortisol keeps being released.

A lot of stress research focuses on cortisol because it can cross the blood-brain barrier and bind to brain regions, including some of those which are crucial to the stress system being activated in the first place, as well as those that help us to control, or regulate, our stress responses and reactions to stress. If our stress systems are activated over a longer period of time, this can make us more vulnerable to new stressful events, creating a negative spiral. Additionally, it can reduce the production of hormones and neurotransmitters which help to reduce or regulate stress responses.

All this is even more important when we are talking about children. Studies on other animal species have shown that young organisms respond more negatively to cortisol. In adult organisms, cortisol helps the body to adapt, but it does not do this to the same degree in young organisms. Instead, it causes more damage to their systems. We believe this same difference exists in humans.

Why? In children, we see that they can develop a type of chronic stress which is more difficult to heal, and it can contribute to mental and physical illnesses. We encourage professionals to read about adverse childhood experiences (ACEs) to learn more about this. In autistic children, specifically, we may worry that sensory sensitivities, difficulties with social interactions, and other challenges associated with autism, could contribute significantly to how often the child experiences a stress response, and how intense these stress responses are. The problem this creates is, of course, that if a child is sensitized to certain experiences early in life, it may also impact their ability to develop cognitively, as they otherwise would. This could mean that difficulties in emotion and energy regulation and impaired executive functioning abilities are exacerbated, that language development and social engagement are affected, often inhibited, or any number of other consequences. This is purely speculative at this point in time; however, these would be some of the concerns in relation to severe childhood stress.

## THE HEALTHY NERVOUS SYSTEM

Our nervous system is highly complicated and scientists do not fully understand it at this point in time. However, based on current research, this section will include short and simplified introductions to various parts of the 'healthy nervous system'.

To do that, however, we first need a crash course on the nervous system overall.

Our central nervous system includes the brain – and thus the limbic system, where stress responses are activated – the brain stem and the nerves along our spinal cord. Everything else is referred to as the *peripheral nervous system*.

If you read about the peripheral nervous system, you often see charts of the sympathetic and parasympathetic nervous systems. It is all quite complicated, so to boil it down, Figure 2.1 shows how they are connected. The peripheral nervous system functions as a communication link or 'liaison' between the central nervous system and the body. This includes both sensory signals and motor signals. The motor division of the peripheral nervous system is then divided into the somatic nervous system, which controls voluntary bodily functions, and the *autonomic nervous system*, which controls involuntary bodily functions. Finally, the autonomic nervous system is then divided into the *sympathetic* and *parasympathetic* nervous systems.

These two systems are always both activated to some degree, but vary in terms of which is 'dominant' at any given time.

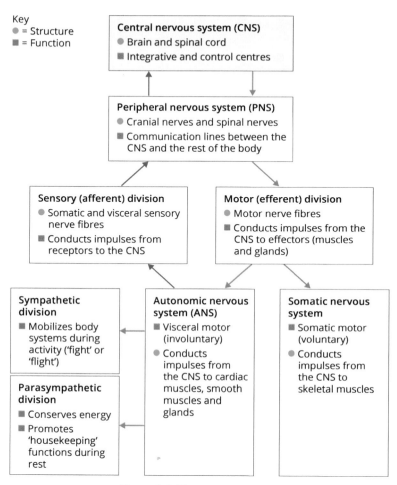

Key
● = Structure
■ = Function

**Central nervous system (CNS)**
● Brain and spinal cord
■ Integrative and control centres

**Peripheral nervous system (PNS)**
● Cranial nerves and spinal nerves
■ Communication lines between the CNS and the rest of the body

**Sensory (afferent) division**
● Somatic and visceral sensory nerve fibres
■ Conducts impulses from receptors to the CNS

**Motor (efferent) division**
● Motor nerve fibres
■ Conducts impulses from the CNS to effectors (muscles and glands)

**Sympathetic division**
■ Mobilizes body systems during activity ('fight' or 'flight')

**Parasympathetic division**
■ Conserves energy
■ Promotes 'housekeeping' functions during rest

**Autonomic nervous system (ANS)**
■ Visceral motor (involuntary)
● Conducts impulses from the CNS to cardiac muscles, smooth muscles and glands

**Somatic nervous system**
■ Somatic motor (voluntary)
● Conducts impulses from the CNS to skeletal muscles

*Figure 2.1: The nervous system*

In essence, the sympathetic nervous system arouses the body to expend energy and is generally connected to adrenaline and noradrenaline – and so is very connected to the fight or flight part of a stress response.

The parasympathetic nervous system calms the body and conserves energy. When we feel relaxed and safe, this nervous system is activated to a higher degree than the sympathetic one.

Importantly, both the sympathetic and parasympathetic nervous systems are necessary for our bodies to function optimally. In fact, they work so closely together that when you breathe in, the sympathetic nervous system is activated, and when you breathe out, the parasympathetic nervous system is activated, and one of the ways we see that change is in the change in heart rate that happens naturally as we breathe in and out. The sympathetic nervous system is tied to arousal and therefore stress, but this does not make it 'the bad' nervous system. What it does mean is that continuous over-activation of one, and under-activation of the other, can lead to unwanted consequences. We are looking for balance and for the body to be able to change between each system and utilize both effectively.

## THE CONNECTION TO STRESS AND TRAUMA

According to polyvagal theory, introduced by Stephen Porges, we have three main responses to threat:

- *Social engagement*, where we try to get help, support or comfort from others. This is regulated by the ventral vagal complex – a branch of the vagus nerve, also sometimes called the tenth cranial nerve. At this level of threat, we have conscious control, and can actively seek and receive comfort through the parts of the nervous system that register and respond to social responses from others.
- *Fight or flight*, a more primal system which helps us to run away or fight off the threat. This response is controlled by the sympathetic nervous system.
- *Collapse or freeze*, in which the dorsal vagal complex is activated. This drastically reduces metabolism, heart rate, breathing and digestive function. It is both an emotional and physical shutdown. When this reaction occurs, we see dissociation, fainting, or people can become 'zombie-like', moving slowly or not reacting effectively to their surroundings.

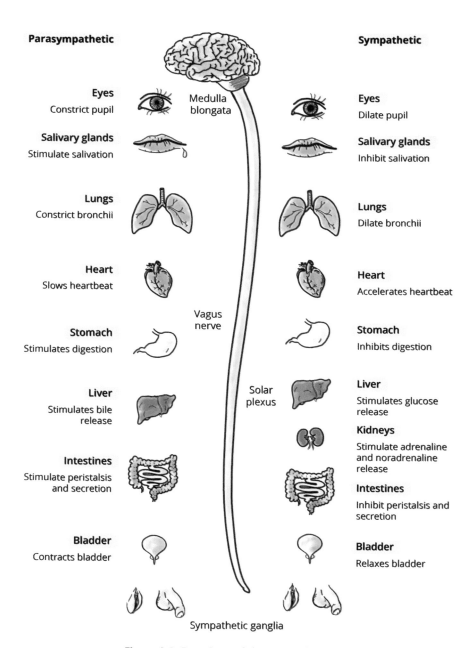

**Parasympathetic**

**Eyes**
Constrict pupil

**Salivary glands**
Stimulate salivation

**Lungs**
Constrict bronchii

**Heart**
Slows heartbeat

**Stomach**
Stimulates digestion

**Liver**
Stimulates bile
release

**Intestines**
Stimulate peristalsis
and secretion

**Bladder**
Contracts bladder

Medulla
blongata

Vagus
nerve

Solar
plexus

Sympathetic ganglia

**Sympathetic**

**Eyes**
Dilate pupil

**Salivary glands**
Inhibit salivation

**Lungs**
Dilate bronchii

**Heart**
Accelerates heartbeat

**Stomach**
Inhibits digestion

**Liver**
Stimulates glucose
release

**Kidneys**
Stimulate adrenaline
and noradrenaline
release

**Intestines**
Inhibit peristalsis and
secretion

**Bladder**
Relaxes bladder

*Figure 2.2: Functions of the sympathetic and
parasympathetic nervous systems*

As you can tell, the vagus nerve, a part of the parasympathetic nervous system, is activated in two of these responses, but with very different results. The collapse or freeze response is the one most associated with psychological trauma, because it is activated when we feel unable to act or are unable to escape the situation. Common examples are when a person is pinned down or threatened into submission by an attacker, a child being stuck in a situation with an abusive caregiver, or when an accident leaves us physically or psychologically unable to move away from the site. It can also be activated when we are unable to protect those we care about.

These activations are connected with the release of stress hormones in the body, and while collapse and freeze responses are often seen in individuals who have PTSD, a single-event trauma, constant smaller threats can still create severe and prolonged stress, such as burnout.

What polyvagal theory teaches us is to remember that stress is not solely in the brain, but rather a complex phenomenon that occurs in the entire body and involves many vital organs, through the nervous system and, centrally, the vagus nerve. This means we can treat stress (and trauma) through therapy, and by helping the body to relearn pleasant activation of the nervous system.

We could go further into the complicated world of the polyvagal theory, but will instead refer interested readers to the work of Stephen Porges (2011).

For now, we want to remember that for the nervous system to work in a healthy way, it must be able to switch between activating the sympathetic and parasympathetic nervous systems rapidly, not over-activating either, and certainly not getting 'stuck' in any activation, especially not in that dorsal-ventral complex, the collapse or freeze reaction.

## PROMOTING RESILIENCE

While we cannot necessarily prepare for or avoid those stressors that cause PTSD for someone – and it can be very hard to avoid burnout or other long-term stress conditions when they are stuck in situations in life where the demands outweigh their resources or capacity – what we can do is promote resilience.

How? We try to give the brain and body the best foundation for healing and maintaining a healthy nervous system, and we purposefully do our best to create an environment for the person which gives access to both rest and recovery, and successfully meeting the challenges that allow them to regain confidence in their own ability and capacity to cope with stressors.

Healthy nervous systems have a good balance of many different neurotransmitters. Balance in neurotransmitters is important, as an overload of one, or, lack of others, leads to unwanted consequences in our mental and physical health. For example, too much dopamine is linked to poor impulse control, as well as increased aggression and competitiveness (Health Direct 2023).

Some neurotransmitters are more easily 'hacked' than others, through our behaviours and even through our diet. This is important for Energy Accounting because it gives us access to making changes to achieve a more balanced nervous system without medical intervention.

● **SEE RESOURCE 3:** *A Guide to Neurotransmitters.*

## CLINICAL VIEW OF STRESS

The term 'stress disorder' is commonly associated with PTSD, where the stress is of an acute traumatic nature. In the *Diagnostic and Statistical Manual of Mental Disorders-5* (DSM-5) and the *International Classification of Diseases* (ICD) diagnostic systems, there are different stress diagnoses, but they primarily describe stress brought on by a single traumatic event or stress caused by life changes.

However, in the clinical world, we do talk about burnout. Burnout is not a diagnosis at this time, but it is a clinical reality to those who experience or work with it. Burnout is usually talked about as a result of work-related chronic stress, and the symptoms are to do with exhaustion, cynicism and lack of efficacy. For some adults, clinical experience, as well as some research, suggests that there is also parental burnout to consider, especially for parents with children who have complex support needs.

What we see in people with burnout is a wide range of symptoms (common ones are listed later in this chapter), some of which overlap with anxiety and depression. People experiencing burnout describe feeling constant fatigue, feeling unable to cope with daily tasks, and experiencing changes to their mood or temper.

Clinically, we see that these symptoms subside over time when the stress or burnout is treated, often by environmental and support changes, but we also see that people who have been in burnout once can be more susceptible to burnout relapse. It seems that there is an increased sensitivity to stressors. This is also the case with depression, as people who have had one clinical depression are more likely to develop depression again later in life.

Based on this knowledge, what we hope to do with Energy Accounting is to provide a method to help people visually track and reflect on their stress and well-being, and hopefully prevent future burnout.

## CONSEQUENCES OF STRESS

The two previous sections have covered this subject to some degree; however, the consequences of stress really are wide-ranging and serious for mental and physical health.

There are serious symptoms in mental health which range from existential crises, feeling that nothing matters anymore, or feeling disconnected from the world, one's own body and its signals, to mood symptoms such as being more prone to emotional outbursts, irritability, sadness or even lack of emotion.

Physical symptoms are also common. These include temporary but reoccurring headaches, dizziness and stomach aches. Heart palpitations are also very common, and may be noticeable throughout the day. You will find more physical symptoms in the table later in this chapter. Note, however, that symptoms can often be difficult to classify as purely physical, psychological or behavioural, as they often affect each area significantly. Memory problems, for example, are a psychological symptom, but may be caused by cortisol damage to the hippocampus and other brain structures – as such, they have a long-term physiological cause or component, and are not solved by therapy alone. Likewise, behavioural symptoms such as self-isolation often have their cause in psychological symptoms such as anxiety, depression or fatigue, which means the person feels that they have no energy for being social. Stress can also affect overall health, both short term and long term. In chronic stress, we often see chronic pain or other chronic illnesses being exacerbated, or even beginning.

Social consequences differ from individual to individual; however, the result is often loneliness. Irritability, anger, cynicism, sadness, depression and anxiety are all factors that can contribute to a person's social life diminishing, in part because the person themselves may be withdrawing from others, but also because others withdraw from them. Additionally, as mentioned, the fatigue or exhaustion associated with stress can mean that the person feels that they have no energy to socialize. Fewer positive social experiences, in turn, exacerbate any existing depression and stress, as the positive emotions (and neurotransmitters and hormones) that they would otherwise get from socializing are now missing. Thus what might otherwise be a buffer against stress becomes less available, and a negative stress spiral can begin.

When we talk about stress, we often talk about losing productivity or efficacy in a professional capacity or within one's personal life. People feel unable to meet the demands set by their environment, and they may 'run themselves into the ground' trying. This can also mean that people feel they have failed in some way, that they are not good enough, and this can lead to considerable feelings of shame.

Part of this shame is related to the societal idea that we, as people, are only worth as much as we are able to produce or accomplish. The idea is that we have to 'earn our keep'. Our sense of self-worth can be tied to how well we live up to other people's expectations of us – other people, society as a whole, or our perception of their expectations. This means that when we find ourselves lacking the ability, resilience or 'strength' to live up to those expectations, our self-worth takes a major blow. This is, in part, what can lead to depression as a symptom of stress.

And we do become less productive when we are stressed, but it is not our fault. We know from the biology of stress that when we are feeling under pressure for a prolonged period of time or to an intense degree, the hormones and neurotransmitters we need to be functional, become unbalanced. There is excess cortisol produced, and over time this can cause damage to brain structures which makes it harder for 'good' neurotransmitters to flow as needed. It is this biological imbalance that causes fatigue, the feeling that nothing really matters, the inability to 'just get things done', and much more. The impact all of this has on productivity is a consequence of biology and illness – productivity dips should not be seen as the fault of the individual. They are not simply down to laziness or lack of resilience. We also know that, at the societal level, stress is one of the costliest illnesses or disorders to the community. It is very difficult to truly quantify the societal costs, as a part of what makes stress so expensive to society is all the invisible costs around it – the mental illnesses that often accompany stress, such as anxiety and depression, the long-term health and employment consequences, and so on. It is not the treating of stress in itself which is expensive, but all the rest. This means that on a societal level, it makes sense to do something to alleviate stress, and it makes sense to do it as early as possible.

It also makes sense on an individual level, of course, because, quite frankly, no one wants to be stressed.

This is all very general, and the individual consequences of stress are sometimes hard to see, especially if a person has been stressed for a long time. They may not remember what it is like to be in a state of well-being. They may not remember life without stress. Stress has become their 'normal'.

Many people may not realize they are experiencing clinical levels of stress until their body begins to shut down, and often it is the physical symptoms they first recognize. They may think they have – or have developed – a heart problem, or a stomach problem. It is a physician rather than a psychologist or psychiatrist who confirms the physiological consequences of chronic stress.

It is important, however, that we address the problem of stress, because a person's life can be affected in many ways, and the effects can become lifelong, and life-threatening, where they need not be if stress is reduced or adequately managed.

Again, we reiterate that Energy Accounting should not be a standalone intervention if there are medical or clinical disorders involved which need medical, psychopharmacological or other therapeutic interventions. If there are medical problems involved, do see a medical professional.

## SYMPTOMS OF STRESS

In previous sections, we have briefly introduced some of the common causes of stress and burnout. Here we provide an overview of common symptoms. This can be useful for reflecting on what you or your clients may be experiencing, which is important both for knowing the warning signs of stress for the future and for periodically evaluating stress levels and progress.

It is important to remember that these symptoms should be viewed and judged against the individual person's 'normal' way of being. For example, social isolation as a symptom should be evaluated in the context of how that person acts when they are not stressed (provided they even know) not against a societal norm or expectation. An autistic person may not perceive themselves to be socially isolated if they see someone every two weeks for a movie night. This may well be their preferred level of socializing, and expectations that they should socialize more could add to stress rather than contribute to well-being.

It is also very important to note that some of these symptoms – especially physical ones – can be symptoms of medical problems as well. Do make sure that any medical causes are investigated before attributing the symptom purely to stress.

As a user of Energy Accounting, the following overview can be used for reflection on your own symptoms, but we also encourage speaking to a professional or a close confidant during this process, as many people can have a hard time noticing their own stress symptoms. It can also be important, over time, to reflect on whether anxiety and/or depression is a symptom of stress or a separate, perhaps pre-existing issue which adds to the stress you are dealing with. The approach to dealing with anxiety and/or depression differs depending on whether it is a symptom of stress or a separate challenge.

One thing to reflect on is which symptoms you may be more able to notice as they develop or diminish. These can function as markers in evaluating progress, and in monitoring well-being. There is more on this point in Chapter 4, Monitoring Well-Being.

As you go through the table, you may want to highlight or write down symptoms that are relevant to you. You can use the provided space to do so, or download a PDF from EnergyAccounting.com/handouts.

Note the symptoms and descriptions that apply to you. Examples could be that there is an increase in a specific type of headache, that you withdraw from certain people, that you tend to forget specific types of information, etc.

*Stress symptoms*

| Physical | Psychological | Outward or behavioural |
|---|---|---|
| Headaches | Diminished interest or pleasure, anhedonia | Insomnia, difficulty sleeping |
| Heart palpitations | Tiredness | Hyperventilation |
| Hands shaking or sweating | Feelings of unease | Feeling overwhelmed by everyday experiences and tasks |
| Dizziness | Memory problems | Self-isolation or becoming socially withdrawn |
| Chest tightness | Difficulty concentrating | Anger |
| Stomach pain | Restlessness | Aggression |
| Frequent urination | Irritability | Decreased productivity or performance |
| Pains | Low self-esteem or self-worth* | Indetermination or indecisiveness |
| Decreased sex drive | Anxiety, panic attacks | Increased use of stimulants (such as caffeine and sugar) |
| Frequent infections | Exhaustion or fatigue | Comfort eating |
| Exacerbation of chronic illness | Affected, changed or diminished sense of humour | Altered dietary habits |
| Teeth grinding | Depression | Excessive sleeping |
| Heartburn | Feeling overwhelmed | Obsessive or compulsive behaviours |
| Nausea | Negativity | Increased number of sick days |
| Weight gain or weight loss | *Increase in negative thoughts about self, for example in terms of personality traits, expectations for the future, or one's appearance. | Skin picking or hair pulling |

It is possible to note acute stress symptoms and longer-term stress symptoms separately. Many of the symptoms noted above tend to be longer-term symptoms, but some can also be acute. Acute stress symptoms are those that appear suddenly – over the course of hours or days – and may only last a short time, such as an outburst lasting minutes, or insomnia lasting a few days.

*Acute stress symptoms*

| Physical | Psychological | Outward or behavioural |
| --- | --- | --- |
| Headache | Difficulty concentrating | Insomnia, difficulty sleeping |
| Heart palpitations | Tiredness | Hyperventilation |
| Hands shaking | Feelings of unease | Feeling overwhelmed by everyday experiences and tasks |
| Dizziness | Restlessness | Self-isolation or becoming socially withdrawn |
| Chest tightness | Irritability | Anger |
| Stomach pain | Panic attack | Aggression |
| Sweaty hands or feet | Meltdown or shutdown | Decreased productivity or performance |
| Nausea | Feeling overwhelmed | Indecisiveness |
| | Negativity | Increased use of stimulants (such as coffee and sugar) |
| | Affected/changed or diminished sense of humour | Comfort eating |
| | Increased desire/craving for sugar/high fat/ unhealthy foods | Sudden (increase in) obsessive or compulsive behaviours |
| | Acute thoughts of self-harm or suicide | |

## My stress symptoms

Note here what your symptoms of stress are from the above list and any that we have not included. If you prefer, it can be useful to try to come up with separate lists for acute and long-term stress symptoms.

. . . . . . . . . . . . . . . . . . . . . . . . . . . . . . . . . . . . . . . . . . . . . . . . . . . . . . . .

. . . . . . . . . . . . . . . . . . . . . . . . . . . . . . . . . . . . . . . . . . . . . . . . . . . . . . . .

. . . . . . . . . . . . . . . . . . . . . . . . . . . . . . . . . . . . . . . . . . . . . . . . . . . . . . . .

. . . . . . . . . . . . . . . . . . . . . . . . . . . . . . . . . . . . . . . . . . . . . . . . . . . . . . . .

. . . . . . . . . . . . . . . . . . . . . . . . . . . . . . . . . . . . . . . . . . . . . . . . . . . . . . . .

. . . . . . . . . . . . . . . . . . . . . . . . . . . . . . . . . . . . . . . . . . . . . . . . . . . . . . . .

. . . . . . . . . . . . . . . . . . . . . . . . . . . . . . . . . . . . . . . . . . . . . . . . . . . . . . . .

. . . . . . . . . . . . . . . . . . . . . . . . . . . . . . . . . . . . . . . . . . . . . . . . . . . . . . . .

. . . . . . . . . . . . . . . . . . . . . . . . . . . . . . . . . . . . . . . . . . . . . . . . . . . . . . . .

. . . . . . . . . . . . . . . . . . . . . . . . . . . . . . . . . . . . . . . . . . . . . . . . . . . . . . . .

. . . . . . . . . . . . . . . . . . . . . . . . . . . . . . . . . . . . . . . . . . . . . . . . . . . . . . . .

. . . . . . . . . . . . . . . . . . . . . . . . . . . . . . . . . . . . . . . . . . . . . . . . . . . . . . . .

. . . . . . . . . . . . . . . . . . . . . . . . . . . . . . . . . . . . . . . . . . . . . . . . . . . . . . . .

. . . . . . . . . . . . . . . . . . . . . . . . . . . . . . . . . . . . . . . . . . . . . . . . . . . . . . . .

● **SEE RESOURCE 4**: *Treatment and Recovery from Stress.*

● **SEE RESOURCE 5**: *Defining Well-Being.*

# CHAPTER 3

## *Well-Being with Autism*

Autistic well-being can take many forms, all depending on each person's individual circumstances. Indeed, all people are unique. Nevertheless, we are also very similar. For this reason, many people will relate to some of the points included in this chapter, such as having a feeling of purpose. However, certain groups of people may experience additional barriers to achieving a feeling of purpose – or other aspects of well-being – due in part to discrimination from their surroundings. This will apply to people with disabilities, diagnoses, or other challenges that exacerbate difficulties in their lives.

With all this in mind, we do still encourage people to remember that when it comes to well-being, we are similar in more ways than we are different – we are all human, after all.

In examining well-being with autism, we see that certain themes seem to emerge consistently. First, well-being seems to be connected with the person's view of their autistic identity – a positive view of autism as a part of one's identity is associated with increased well-being.

Second, the level of support and understanding someone receives from their surroundings is connected with well-being. This is fairly self-evident and applies to all people. Having support and understanding from friends and family is important for everyone, no matter who you are and what your challenges and strengths may be.

With regard to autism, research often defines quality of life in a certain way, especially in outcome studies. These are studies which attempt to figure out which factors in an autistic person's life contribute to a 'better future' for that person. That better future – the outcome – is often defined in these contexts as having steady employment, a partner or spouse, children and regular social interactions. But when working with autistic people, can we truly say that these factors are what define a good life? The definitions suggested by non-autistic people may not apply, and may indeed be harmful to achieving a better quality of life for autistic people.

Our goals with Energy Accounting align, perhaps, with the ideas held by proponents of neurodiversity, recognizing and respecting neurological differences as human variations. We wish to work towards the best possible functional daily life that the person can achieve at any given time.

Naturally, when we use a phrase like 'functional daily life', we again need to specify what is meant as it could be misinterpreted. When phrases such as these are used in this book, they imply 'what works for this particular person and contributes to their well-being'. That is, we are not suggesting that any person's functional daily life should emulate cultural standards for how to live. Rather, their functional daily life is one that matches their needs, resources, energy and abilities at that given time.

Research suggests that autistic people who focus on activities that bring pleasure and a sense of fulfilment for them, rather than conforming to society's standards and expectations, have a more successful outcome in terms of well-being and quality of life, in the context of improved mental health and general happiness. This again seems self-evident. It should not be a point that needs to be made. However, for many years, the trend has been to wish that autistic people seek outcomes in lifestyle that mimic those of non-autistic people, or even to push them towards these. Unfortunately, this often leads to more stress, anxiety and depression for autistic people, and, naturally, this is what we wish to avoid.

Recent research on ageing and autism suggests that mature (over the age of 60) autistic adults have discovered well-being strategies themselves through reading, information on the internet, and conversations with other mature autistic adults. Activities such as gardening, craft and hobbies and achieving self-acceptance and a sense of humour contributed to improved mental health (Ommensen 2023).

From personal and clinical experience, we suggest the following as ideas for factors contributing to well-being and quality of life for the autistic person.

## TIME SPENT ON SPECIAL INTERESTS

According to the *DSM-5* Text Revision (2022), having a history of intense interests is one of the diagnostic criteria for autism (TR B3, p.57). The interest is diagnostically significant when it is unusual in terms of intensity or focus. In diagnostic language, these interests are often discussed in a way which puts them in a negative light. While at this point in time some may prefer other terms for these interests, the prevailing and popularized term is 'special interest'. Clinical experience and autistic people's own testimonies suggests that the interest(s) provides the greatest source of joy and fulfilment available for many autistic people. Because of how central these interests are to the experience of prolonged positive emotions and energy, many autistic people describe access to and time spent on their special interest as being important to their sense of overall happiness, self-identity and well-being.

While it is important that the interest does not overshadow other parts of a person's life to the extent that it prevents them from having independence in their daily lives – performing daily tasks, being social in a way that is meaningful for them, keeping a steady sleeping rhythm, and so on – it is equally important to recognize the contribution that the special interest makes to their lives.

The interest may at times be the only activity that seems meaningful or joyful to the person, and activities associated with the interest can be so pure as a source of joy that they temporarily remove or block symptoms of depression, anxiety and stress. Likewise, the interest may be used as a part of a psychological treatment programme, exactly because of the joy associated with it. The interest can encourage social interaction as well, because the person is so enthusiastic regarding the interest that they wish to meet and share their knowledge and passion with others. In this way, the special interest presents a gateway to social activity with those who share the interest.

Before the introduction of Energy Accounting, the special interest may be primarily a source of enjoyment, but in Energy Accounting, we actively and consciously use the special interest as a tool to reduce stress. This means simultaneously protecting and maintaining the haven that it provides. If the person perceives that their time spent on the interest is *only* provided to the necessary extent required for their daily energy account to achieve balance, this may become a source of sadness and sorrow. Consider the special interest as something sacred. It should be handled with a great deal of respect and care, and restricting access to it must be based in reason and benefit for the autistic person. This is to say, don't restrict access to the special interest to the minimal amount required for the person to function – usually there is no point in restricting access, as long as the person's basic needs are otherwise met.

## SOCIAL INTERACTIONS, QUALITY RATHER THAN QUANTITY

Due to the challenges involved in social interaction, there can be a decreased desire for being social – at least in the sense that non-autistic people tend to be. Many autistic people are happier to engage in social interaction with one or two other people at a time, and to have social interactions take place via the internet, either through social media or online gaming. Often, they prefer social interactions that are *about* something, either a topic or an activity, that creates a framework for the interactions to take place within. Autistic people tend to prefer fewer social interactions than non-autistic people, with key people in their lives and involving topics or activities of importance to them, rather than many social interactions, which they may perceive as shallow, exhausting or unnecessary. Making the choice to engage in the interactions that are more meaningful contributes to feeling happier with the time spent and the people it is spent with – and thus improves well-being.

## LOWERED STRESS, ANXIETY AND DEPRESSION

A key issue for many autistic people is feelings of stress, anxiety and depression. In many cases, though not all, anxiety and depression may even be diagnosed along with autism, as a co-existing disorder. In self-reports of anxiety and depression in autistic people, numbers are as high as 80 per cent, while there is a prevalence of only 5 per cent for the general population (Mattila *et al.* 2010; Van Steensel *et al.* 2011; White *et al.* 2009). There have been studies specifically examining the levels of depression, anxiety and stress in autistic adults. A study by McGillivray and Evert (2018) used the *Depression Anxiety Stress Scales* and more than half the participants reported that they were experiencing mild to extremely severe symptoms of depression (59%), anxiety (56%) and stress (63%). For this reason, many autistic people report that lowered levels of anxiety, depression and stress would improve their well-being and mental health, and even be vital to improving it.

This is, of course, a central part of Energy Accounting but, critically, this focus on lowering levels of anxiety, depression and stress should be both a short- and long-term goal, and should include making sure the person has a range of tools at their disposal for this purpose – a strategy toolbox or library, so to speak.

## HAVING COPING MECHANISMS FOR SENSORY SENSITIVITIES

As autistic people frequently have differences in the way they experience sensory information, many have trouble living their lives without experiencing severe stress due to sensory overload.

Having coping mechanisms available at all times can be a life-changer, especially if there are several options available for different situations. Sometimes this does involve avoidance tactics, while in other situations, it may be simply a matter of having the correct distractions, de-stressing sensory toys, or other sensory inputs that can 'override' the bad ones. A frequently used example of this is using music in headphones to create a sound blanket when the person is in a public space with more noise than they are comfortable with.

## FEELING THAT YOU HAVE PURPOSE

Needing a feeling of purpose in life is something many people, autistic or not, can relate to. The feeling of having purpose may be connected to the special interest, a job, taking care of a pet, or being a positive part of certain people's lives. Whatever it is, this is certainly something to prioritize in the pursuit of improved well-being. People who do not have the feeling that they have purpose in life may be more prone to depression and feelings of apathy. Feeling that you have purpose can contribute to a drive to achieve something, higher self-esteem, and to wanting to take good care of yourself in the long term.

## FEELING OF AGENCY

Agency is a term used in social sciences to describe a person's capability to make choices and actions that have an impact on their lives and the world around them. These can be small, everyday things like being able to choose your bedtime. It can also be about who to socialize with, choosing to pursue a new job, or it can be choices and actions on a societal level, such as being able to vote. The feeling of having agency is tied to different things for people of different ages, but make no mistake: children seek the experience of agency, too.

For children, feeling that they have agency can be tied to having a voice in seemingly small or relatively unimportant things like the choice of dinner, where to go for an outing or what to wear.

However, many children begin to explore their agency by wanting to have choices in who gets to enter their room and when, and controlling what their pocket money is spent on in spite of age-related rules that parents may have set for what the child is allowed to have access to. This isn't about rebellion, but rather emphasizes that people – all people – feel the need to have agency over certain things in their daily life and that having a certain degree of agency is important for well-being.

## STRUCTURE AND CONSISTENCY FOR THE DAY

Whether they know it or not, non-autistic people like structure and consistency, too. However, for autistic people, allowing for increased structure and consistency can be a major way to reduce anxiety and frustration. When we know what to expect, we can spend our energy on other things during the day, rather than adjusting to unforeseen events. This is especially important for autistic people because changes and surprises can trigger high levels of anxiety and discomfort, which is energy draining. As we know, unpredictability and a decreased sense of control are two of the four factors that contribute to stress responses, and with this in mind, structure and consistency as factors in well-being make a lot of sense.

For Energy Accounting, building in structure and consistency is important, but creating options in daily life can be too! For example, knowing in advance that you have two or three choices for breakfast can be a way to break up the tedium for those who get bored with the same foods over time. With regard to adjusting to changes, knowing that if x happens, your solutions can be y or z, can be a factor in decreasing the stress, because your appraisal of the stressor changes. Simply by knowing the options in advance, some flexibility can be built into a person's life in a positive way. However, be mindful that this does not work for everyone.

## SUMMARY

With all of this in mind, it seems clear that well-being and quality of life should be defined individually, with positive regard for the specific needs of each person. This can mean rejecting the social norm of what a good life 'should' look like, and finding alternatives based around the individual's personality, dreams, goals and much more.

For autistic people, there are a number of key factors for increasing well-being and quality of life, some of which may also apply to other groups, such as those with social anxiety, ADHD or sensory processing differences. These include:

- time spent on special interest(s)
- quality rather than quantity with regard to social interactions
- a focus on lowering stress, anxiety and depression in daily life as well as in the long term
- having coping mechanisms for sensory sensitivities
- a feeling of purpose
- a feeling of agency in your life
- structure and consistency or choice and flexibility in day-to-day life
- a positive (autistic) identity
- feeling supported, understood and appreciated.

# CHAPTER 4

# Monitoring Well-Being

Monitoring well-being is a major component of evaluating progress when using Energy Accounting, both when trying to reduce stress and to achieve some stability in stress levels. However, just like everything else in Energy Accounting, it is important to recognize that the process of monitoring well-being must be personalized. This chapter provides a general introduction to how well-being can be monitored, and includes a brief section on how to use monitoring in continual evaluations.

The first thing to note on well-being is that we are not striving for perfection. If someone is scoring how well they feel from 1 to 10, where 10 is as happy and healthy as they could possibly be, hardly anyone would ever be score 10. Even the healthiest people have concerns about their health, fall ill, get injured and so on. Even the happiest people can have bad days, suffer from emotional turmoil or even have mental illness. Being well is not a state of things being constantly fantastic. When using Energy Accounting, we aren't looking for our bodies or minds to reach a standard that is unattainable. We are looking for a realistic level of well-being that the person finds comfortable and that they wish to achieve.

One of the common characteristics of autism is a difficulty perceiving and thus monitoring inner experiences and emotions, including well-being. There may be a challenge with perceiving introspective information on mental states and self-reflection. When someone with autism is asked 'How are you feeling?' there can be a genuine difficulty perceiving, collating and communicating information that determines a sense of well-being. Sometimes another person who knows the autistic person very well, such as a parent or partner, may be more able to 'read' the signals of well-being by observing facial expressions, gestures, actions, tone of voice and aspects of conversation and enjoyment from interests. It is important to listen to their assessment of well-being, which may not be consciously recognized by the autistic person. We are not saying that autistic people cannot be introspective – many can and do. However, *for those who find it challenging*, it may be helpful to include other people's observations in the monitoring process.

## PHYSICAL HEALTH

Some people may have experienced considerable emotional stress for much of their life. This is likely to have had an effect on their physical health in terms of stress-related illnesses such as headaches and migraines, gastro-intestinal disorders and reduced effectiveness of their immune and physical health recovery systems. A measure of stress can be the number of times that a person accesses medical services. Their well-being may have been affected by chronic or intermittent physical illness.

One thing to note is that for autistic people, decreased interoception may be an issue. Interoception refers to the ability to perceive internal sensory signals such as pain, heart rate, breathing, hunger and tiredness. This means that physical health needs to be monitored in ways that are very concrete, such as using a fitness watch, having regular medical check-ups or having a regular 'questionnaire'-type interview with a caregiver or close relation, using very concrete questions about the person's physical health.

Other autistic people have the opposite issue, being extremely sensitive to bodily sensations, possibly having a low threshold for pain or being able to feel slight changes in heart rate very easily. Many have a mixture of the two, where certain sensations are very clear, and others are nearly impossible to notice. That is, it is possible to be both hypo- and hypersensitive to different sensations as well as other forms of input. It would be worthwhile identifying and making a list of which internal bodily signals a person is sensitive to or has difficulty perceiving.

## Daily activity

When someone feels energy depleted there can be considerable difficulty initiating and completing the regular schedule of daily activities. It may become more difficult to manage school or work tasks, as well as tasks in the home. In this sense, what a person achieves in the day can be a measure of well-being. There will be a number of tasks they are able to deal with and get done when they feel well, and usually, as well-being declines, so does the energy for daily activities. Thus, a lack of daily activity is often a sign of energy depletion. Simultaneously, well-being can be affected by having a sense of underachievement, and so this may become a vicious cycle in which not having the energy makes you feel unable to do things, and not having done them makes you feel badly about yourself which in turn affects your ability to complete the tasks you wish to.

## Nourishment (food)

Buying and preparing food requires considerable energy and organizational skills. There can be a temptation to buy junk food that does not require any preparation and cooking time in the kitchen. However, we know from surveys of autistic adults that a significant contribution to a sense of well-being comes from reducing junk food and eating a healthy diet (Attwood, Evans & Lesko 2014).

In monitoring physical health, as well as mental health, how we eat may be an indicator of well-being, but it may also be a way to make very concrete and effective changes to our well-being. Some people may be able to use the frequency with which they buy and consume ready-made foods such as frozen dinners or take-out as an indicator of their well-being, such that when the frequency increases, this means extra energy needs to be allocated to their cooking and diet for a time, in order to restabilize their well-being through physical health initiatives. This is rarely the only change, but we have found that diet can make a vast difference not only to physical health, but also to mental health.

## Hygiene

There can be a sense of well-being created by feeling clean and having good personal hygiene. All animals spend time cleaning themselves, and humans also need to devote time to personal hygiene for well-being and the benefit of others who have an aversive reaction to body odour. We also need to be clean to prevent bacterial infection that affects general health. However, when well-being declines, hygiene habits are often one of the first indicators. We have seen, clinically, that when anxiety, depression or stress begin to take hold, early indicators may be:

- an increase in time between showers/baths
- forgetting or neglecting (not seeing the point) to brush teeth
- a decrease in the amount of time spent grooming, especially hair-brushing or shaving
- paying less attention than usual to clothing, such as wearing the same clothes for days or even weeks at a time.

## Outdoors activity

Our bodies need sunlight to obtain vitamin D and there has been an association between vitamin D deficiency and autism (Cannell 2017). We do not know why this association exists, but it may be that autistic people are less prone to spending time outside due to sensory or social difficulties or a preference to engage in indoor activities. It may feel safer in terms of social and sensory experiences to avoid leaving your home and being outdoors, but as humans we need sunlight to improve and maintain our mental and physical well-being. Daily exposure to sunlight helps to establish natural sleep rhythms, which can be highly beneficial, as lack of sleep and poor sleep quality can be improved by having a regular sleep pattern. There are several approaches to implementing a regular sleep schedule, and there is likely to be a challenge in finding the strategies that work for the individual; however, there is often an immense pay-off in terms of increased well-being when the correct strategies are found.

When well-being is decreasing, there can be an increasing tendency to stay inside. As humans, we seek safety when we feel uncertain or vulnerable, and for many people, safety means home. Autistic people have the additional challenges of possible sensory sensitivities or anxiety about several aspects of being outside. Often, this will be things like the intensity of sunlight, certain frequencies of light, or eyes that are sensitive to wind, making it difficult to see. It can also be social anxiety making it uncomfortable to encounter strangers or crowds, even without interaction. Both anxiety and sensory sensitivities may worsen with increased stress, amplifying the challenges that come with them.

## Lifestyle

A varied lifestyle enhances a sense of well-being. When one activity, regardless of the type of activity, takes up a disproportionate amount of the day and night, there are concerns regarding the lack of diversity in neurotransmitters being introduced. As explained in the section on the healthy nervous system, different neurotransmitters serve different functions, and we need a balance in neurotransmitters to function well. If the activity is sedentary and involves being in one posture for too long, such as sitting at a desk looking at a computer screen, lack of exercise and sunlight can be a concern as well, with long-term effects on physical as well as mental health. If the activity is physically active, such as a fitness activity, or your employment requires considerable and continuous physical exertion, the brain can become used to being overloaded with dopamine and endorphins, or there can be damage done to joints, nerves or muscles. Such damage can be very difficult to treat if the activity is not appropriate to the person's fitness level and age, and if they do not notice any issues in time to seek early treatment.

Generally, however, the human body and mind tends to feel better when everyday life has some variation in activities. Our brains function better when we get access to a balanced amount of different neurotransmitters, which means not getting stuck doing the same thing for too long every day.

Computer gaming is a popular hobby or interest these days, but often people already spend a lot of their day at a desk job or at a school desk. This means many people are not getting much exercise or exposure to natural levels of sunlight, and this can lead to lacking the energy to perform many daily chores. For those who are not using the blue-light blocking technologies that are found in many computers and devices, there is the additional risk of doing harm to the circadian rhythm, and impacting sleep quantity and quality.

## MENTAL HEALTH

Three-quarters of autistic adults have daily concerns with their anxiety, sadness and anger (Attwood *et al.* 2014). There are many neurological, genetic and circumstantial reasons for fluctuating mood and mental health issues for autistic adults. The feelings of anxiety, sadness and anger affect perception and thinking. When feeling anxious, the mind finds many things to worry about, and anxious thoughts can become so intense that an anxiety disorder is diagnosed. Feeling sad can lead to perceiving many current and past experiences as legitimizing pessimism and despair. Clinical depression may be diagnosed when the level of sadness and negativity reaches a critical point. In short, anxiety and sadness can create negative spirals, because the emotions change the way we perceive the world and our own experiences.

Anxiety may be reduced by a range of strategies such as engaging in routines and rituals which are soothing and being totally involved in a special interest as an anxious thought blocker. When prevented from these anxiety-reducing activities there can be a feeling of frustration and pent-up energy that can be expressed as explosive anger. An autistic person feeling sad and despondent may not express depression in a conventional way – that is, internalizing the feelings and engaging in self-blame and guilt with a conspicuous lack of energy – but may explode with energy and anger. The feelings are externalized and the person goes into 'attack mode'.

Worry, sadness and agitation make a sense of well-being more elusive, but treatment for mental health issues can help with this.

We also recognize that stress can increase the characteristics of autism. Family- and friendship-related stress may reduce social engagement and increase repetitive behaviour and interests as well as sensory sensitivity (Kelly *et al.* 2008).

For monitoring mental health, we recommend looking back at the list of stress symptoms, but also including lists of symptoms for anxiety and depression. If possible, the individual should write down which symptoms are more common to them, and when they seem to occur. However, it can be difficult to remember during 'good' periods how it feels during the bad ones. For that reason, writing a journal can be very effective. For the person, keeping track of how they feel, how well they are, over time, may help to reveal which symptoms are most relevant, and which may be the first ones to appear.

## List of symptoms, anxiety and depression
This list includes both clinical symptoms and brief general descriptions of the experience, which may be easier to understand for the lay person.

If you are using this book as a self-help guide or in preparation for a session with a mental health professional or support person, you may go through the following exercise. Can you identify three to five symptoms from these lists which may be early indicators for you? If you can, do have a support person, friend, family member or carer with you to discuss these indicators as they may be helpful in recalling past mental health declines, as well as monitoring mental health for the future.

On a piece of paper, write down your symptoms.

| Anxiety (as there are many different anxiety diagnoses, we are focusing on generalized anxiety here, and supplementing with additional information) | Depression |
|---|---|
| • Excessive anxiety and worry, more days than not. (Feelings of anxiousness and worrying that do not match the person's actual life situation, meaning, the feelings are unrealistic or irrational)<br>• Difficulty controlling the worry<br>• Restlessness, feeling keyed up or on edge<br>• Being easily fatigued<br>• Difficulty concentrating, or the mind going blank<br>• Irritability<br>• Muscle tension<br>• Sleep disturbance (difficulty falling or staying asleep, or restless, unsatisfying sleep)<br>• Panic attacks (which can include trembling or shaking, feelings of choking, nausea, dizziness, numbness, fear of losing control or 'going crazy', fear of dying, etc.)<br>• Social anxiety, marked by fear or anxiety about social situations which can involve possible scrutiny by others<br>• Fears of acting in a way others will judge (being embarrassed or humiliated)<br>• Avoidance of social situations<br>• Separation anxiety, with excessive distress when the person anticipates or experiences separation from home or attachment figures (often parents)<br>• Persistent, excessive worry about losing attachment figures, or them being harmed, becoming ill, and so on<br>• Nightmares involving separation<br>• Persistent, excessive worry about getting separated from attachment figures due to an event, such as being kidnapped, getting lost, or having an accident | • Depressed mood for most of the day, nearly every day (can also be irritable)<br>• Diminished pleasure or interest in all, or almost all, activities – again most of the day, nearly every day<br>• Significant weight loss without attempts at dieting, OR weight gain<br>• Insomnia or hypersomnia nearly every day (difficulty falling asleep, or sleeping in extreme amounts)<br>• Psychomotor agitation or retardation nearly every day (the person moves in a restless way, or quicker than usual, or appears to be slowed down or moves less than usual)<br>• Fatigue or loss of energy nearly every day<br>• Feelings of worthlessness or excessive or inappropriate guilt (i.e. guilt that does not make sense for the person's situation, not 'just' being self-reproachful)<br>• Feelings of hopelessness<br>• Diminished ability to think or concentrate, indecisiveness, nearly every day<br>• Recurrent thoughts of death, suicidal ideation without a specific plan or suicide attempt, or making specific plans for committing suicide |

## PERCEIVED ENERGY

We all, to some extent, have days where we feel more or less energized. Mental energy can naturally be 'tidal'. For some people, this follows a very noticeable pattern, and for others it is harder to spot the ups and downs in general energy levels.

Most people tend to notice that energy levels are higher at the start of the day. Some people feel less energized in the mornings, but after a shower, breakfast, coffee or simply getting out of the door, their perceived energy level increases. For many people, there may be a distinct energy pattern to the week. Often, this includes starting the week with more perceived energy, and around Wednesday or Thursday, there is noticeably less energy in the morning. Then, during the weekend, a 'recharging' or 'saving' of energy occurs, and the next week begins again at a higher level of perceived energy.

When someone feels more energized, they are often able to cope with more events, or may simply be in a better mood. People react in different ways to having less energy. However, our point in tracking this is to find out when and where the energy is spent. It can also be helpful later on, when we look at which changes may be beneficial to make in daily or weekly schedules.

So how do we track a person's perceived energy and energy pattern?

### *Tracking ideas*

There are several ways to measure and track energy levels. It is really up to the individual. One option is to have a numerical rating from zero (no energy) to five or ten when energy is abundant. The numerical rating for stages in the day from early morning to late evening may indicate an energy 'rhythm' to the day. Another option is to have a colour-coding system using the colours the person feels best represent different levels of energy. Often people use the colours of the traffic light, such that green is abundant energy, yellow is a middle ground, and red means depleted.

On occasion, someone might want to use other methods such as descriptive word lists or 'grades'. Here are some variations we have seen suggested:

| | | | |
|---|---|---|---|
| Perfect | Energized | ++ | A |
| Great | Happy | + | B |
| Good | Content | - | C |
| (Meh) | Sad | -- | D |
| Bad | Frustrated | | E |
| Awful | Angry or Irritable | | F |
| | Stressed | | |
| | Anxious | | |
| | Depressed | | |

However, we want to caution against any method that causes a person to feel that a day was 'good' or 'bad'. What we are attempting to track is the level of energy the person has throughout the day, not whether they were satisfied with the day on an emotional level. With grading methods, there is a distinct risk that the person may end up tracking how 'well' they feel they did that day, or how many bad things happened, rather than focusing on their perceived energy levels. Perceived energy and emotion do influence one another, but they are not the same, and we would not want to conflate them as this could increase anxiety, depression or poor self-esteem.

Here are some examples of what it could look like to implement a tracking system across the week.

*Number tracking*

| Day | Monday | Tuesday | Wednesday | Thursday | Friday | Saturday | Sunday |
|---|---|---|---|---|---|---|---|
| Morning | 9 | 7 | 7 | 6 | 4 | 4 | 8 |
| Midday | 5 | 6 | 5 | 4 | 3 | 4 | 8 |
| Evening | 3 | 3 | 3 | 1 | 1 | 6 | 7 |
| Night | 3 | 5 | 4 | 1 | 1 | 5 | 7 |

*Battery tracking*

| Day | Monday | Tuesday | Wednesday | Thursday | Friday | Saturday | Sunday |
|---|---|---|---|---|---|---|---|
| Morning | | | | | | | |
| Midday | | | | | | | |
| Evening | | | | | | | |
| Night | | | | | | | |

*Figure 4.1: Battery tracking*

Another form of tracking, which can provide more detailed information and is often used in therapeutic settings, is inspired by the
CAT-kit,[1] and shows a day horizontally. We track along with the
time of day, but because of the format there is more space to add
details about what happened during each timeframe that might
have influenced energy levels. Here is an example:

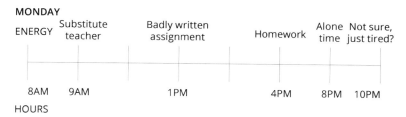

*Figure 4.2: Time-code tracking*

Note that it is not necessary to fill in information for every hour of
the day. Instead, you choose what information is relevant to add.

---

1   Psychologists use the kit for cognitive behaviour therapy with autistic children,
    young people and adults. The CAT-kit provides a visual structure that can be
    used to clarify, achieve self-insight, communicate personal experiences and
    identify new, appropriate ways of communicating thoughts and feelings. The
    kit is currently available in a printed version at https://cat-kit.com/en-gb.

The monitoring ideas included here can be used in a physical calendar or bullet journal, but you can also find downloadable files on energyaccounting.com.

## MONITORING SYMPTOMS OF STRESS AND WELL-BEING

An important part of monitoring well-being is to regularly monitor and track the symptoms of stress and well-being. It is perhaps strange to talk about *symptoms* of well-being, because this is not normally how we talk about feeling content or positive. However, there are signs that someone is well, just as there are signs that they are unwell. It can be difficult to recognize symptoms of well-being, precisely because we do not often – as a society – discuss what well-being actually is or how it feels. As a part of Energy Accounting, we do encourage a discovery of well-being symptoms, as this will contribute to increased self-understanding and provide more of a focus on what increased quality of life may be for the individual.

Because it is often easier, we can begin again by examining stress symptoms.

*Stress symptoms*

| Physical | Psychological | Outward or behavioural |
|---|---|---|
| Headaches | Diminished interest or pleasure, anhedonia | Insomnia, difficulty sleeping |
| Heart palpitations | Tiredness | Hyperventilation |
| Hands shaking or sweating | Feelings of unease | Feeling overwhelmed by everyday experiences and tasks |
| Dizziness | Memory problems | Self-isolation or becoming socially withdrawn |
| Chest tightness | Difficulty concentrating | Anger |
| Stomach pain | Restlessness | Aggression |

| Frequent urination | Irritability | Decreased productivity or performance |
|---|---|---|
| Pains | Low self-esteem or self-worth* | Indetermination or indecisiveness |
| Decreased sex drive | Anxiety, panic attacks | Increased use of stimulants (such as caffeine and sugar) |
| Frequent infections | Exhaustion or fatigue | Comfort eating |
| Exacerbation of chronic illness | Affected, changed or diminished sense of humour | Altered dietary habits |
| Teeth grinding | Depression | Excessive sleeping |
| Heartburn | Feeling overwhelmed | Obsessive or compulsive behaviours |
| Nausea | Negativity | Increased number of sick days |
| Weight gain or weight loss | *Increase in negative thoughts about self, for example in terms of personality traits, expectations for the future, or one's appearance. | Skin picking or hair pulling |

Note also that symptoms such as lack of concentration or rest-lessness can take forms you may not expect. Some autistic people, when stressed or lacking energy, want to dive into special interests but are so desperate for the recharging effects that they attempt to multitask with the special interests – for example, playing a computer game while watching a documentary on a topic they enjoy. This often doesn't have the same recharging effect as allowing themselves to hyper-focus on just one interest at a time. Additionally, when stressed, it can be much more difficult to hyper-focus due to loss of concentration, which makes recharging more difficult. In such a case, it can be beneficial to practise only doing one thing at a time (the game *or* the documentary). The person may only be able to focus for short periods of time on that one thing, but it can help them over time to get back to a healthier way of coping with the stress they feel. In effect, engaging in special interests can be seen as a mindfulness activity, and you cannot multitask mindfulness – it defeats the purpose.

As noted, symptoms of well-being are often harder to identify for people, especially when they are feeling stressed, anxious or depressed. In many cases, it is easiest to begin by flipping stress symptoms, and examining what the reverse might be.

Here is a table you can use for inspiration, with examples of symptoms we often see in our clinical work. Note that the physical symptoms are not included in this table, because they are often simply the absence of physical stress symptoms.

*Well-being symptoms*

| Psychological | Outward or behavioural |
| --- | --- |
| Finding it easy or less challenging to initiate tasks | Laughs easily/more humour |
| Stability in mood (extreme negative emotions are rare) | Spontaneous activities happen more often, or are not experienced as very stressful |
| Having an easier time letting go of negative emotions (they mostly pass within 7–20 minutes) | Sings to oneself |
| Wanting to socialize | Hygiene routines are kept with relative ease |
| Feeling able to relax | Good quality sleep most nights |
| Living 'in the moment', not worrying about the future or ruminating about the past | |
| Optimism | |
| Feeling comfortable with own identity | |
| Feeling mentally and physically energized | |

If you are using this book as a self-help guide or in preparation to seeing a mental health professional or support person, you can use the following exercise: What are your internal signs of well-being and stress that you recognize within yourself and the external signs recognized by others? You may use the table of symptoms as a starting point if it is difficult to get started.

| | Internal | External |
|---|---|---|
| Positive symptoms (well-being symptoms) | | |
| Negative symptoms (stress symptoms or signs of overload) | | |

● **SEE RESOURCE 6**: *Monitoring by Others.*

## SELF-MONITORING

There are several ways to go about self-monitoring, and it is quite possible there are many others not noted here. If you or your client has an idea not mentioned here, do try those out. It is important to find ways that work for each person.

Simply having a system to note down 'How do I feel?' perhaps at the start and end of the day, or even once a day, can be a great way to self-monitor. A numerical scale of well-being that ranges from 1 to 100 or 1 to 10 can be useful. For the scale of 1–100, for example, the natural or neutral state of well-being could be rated as 50, so that numbers below 50 indicate a lower sense of well-being and above 50 a greater sense of well-being. Make a note of the numerical value of well-being at the start and end of the day and perhaps at specific times during the day. These types of scales can also be used for depression symptoms, perceived energy or other factors it would be helpful to track. Obviously, specific events or circumstances affect the numerical rating, such as being very late for work due to traffic delays or having a severe cold. However, an underlying trend can still be identified accommodating unusual events and circumstances.

Having particular, preferably concrete, stress symptoms described makes them easier to notice. Also, having 'rules' about when something needs to change can be useful (i.e. 'When I begin to forget to brush my teeth before bed, this means my energy levels are too low and I need to re-evaluate').

When we keep track of our routine or perceived energy, we may notice that certain changes are warning signs of decreasing well-being. Very often, changes in diet or hygiene routines can be signs of acutely low stress capacity, and if these changes persist, they may be warning signs of increased stress, anxiety or depression.

There are some benefits from fitness watches for acute monitoring, as they monitor heart rate, which can be an indication of heightened emotional states – when it isn't due to exercise of course. Some sports watches can create a graph of heart rate throughout the day or over a period of time, which can provide very valuable information.

If someone discovers they are prone to cyclical changes in their stress capacity, it may be very useful to track the lows and highs on a calendar. Having the pattern physically in front of you can make it easier to spot, so make sure the calendar year is fully visible with this information showing while evaluating or during monitoring sessions.

## Tides of autism or mood (mood diary)

When our stress capacity is lower, for whatever reason, our mood is influenced and things we are usually able to cope well with seem more difficult. This has been called the 'tides of autism'. At times, it may seem as if there is no obvious cause, and at others there is a clear reason why. From what we see in our work, a 'change in the tides' is often the result of sensory or social overload, whether affecting mood, exhaustion or hormonal changes.

### Keeping an autism or mood diary

On some days, the 'tide' of autism may be high; the individual is likely to feel less able to cope with social experiences, sensory sensitivity will be greater and so will anxiety or depression. For everyone, feelings of sadness tend to fluctuate from day to day as a reaction to specific events, but these can also fluctuate according to internal cycles, or 'tides', of depression. This can be an under-lying sadness that is not simply a reaction to events in life, but slowly gathering feelings of low mood over days, weeks or months.

Keeping an autism or mood diary helps to record daily levels of overall mood to forewarn of any mood or depression cycles. The process is very simple and can provide invaluable data to prevent a relapse into depression.

At the end of each day, the individual reflects on how they felt throughout the day. They consider whether their adverse/ unwanted symptoms of autism, anxiety or depression were increased compared to an average day, or whether their mood was different, perhaps even feeling out of context. The degree or depth of adverse autism, anxiety or depression symptoms can be measured using a numerical rating of 0–20, with 10 being the usual or default experience of these symptoms; 0–9 would be an indication that the experience of symptoms was less unpleasant than usual, and 11–20 would be more symptoms than usual, or more severe symptoms than usual.

Using depression as an example, with a numerical rating of 0–20, 0–9 would be the sad to depression range, with 0 being feelings of severe depression and 9 being just a little down or morose; 11–20 would be the happy range, with 11 being a little more content than usual and 20 being a sense of euphoria. If it feels more comfortable, flip the scale around, such that severity of symptoms increases with numerical value – this works just as well, and as long as you know what you are tracking and how, you will get information from it over time.

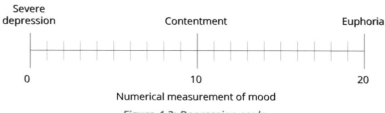

*Figure 4.3: Depression scale*

Decide the single numerical rating that measures the overall level or position on the dimension of sadness to happiness for the day. Record that level of autism, anxiety, or depression symptoms in a diary and then create a chart or graph with the horizontal axis being time (days) and the vertical axis being the rating (0–20). Gradually, a pattern or trend may become apparent that can indicate that the symptoms are increasing and, for example, a relapse into depression is impending. It will be necessary to refresh the energy accounting strategies to resist and protect against becoming more depressed again.

It is important to record the severity of symptoms over time. It takes only a moment to use the above scale, and engaging in this quick and simple activity can act as a cue to begin emotional repair or plan more energy-restoring activities to alleviate a potential aggravation of adverse symptoms.

There may be some concerns regarding the cyclical extremes of mood using the numerical scale above. We have focused on cyclical depression, but there may be cyclical euphoria that reaches a level of clinical concern and recognition of the characteristics of bipolar 11 disorder, with periods of hypomania. There are specific psychiatric and psychological treatments for bipolar 11 disorder.

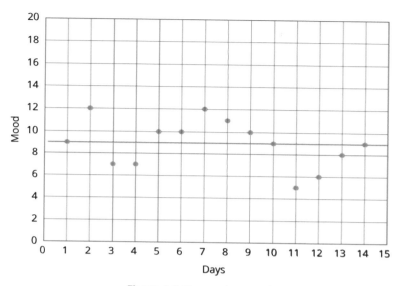

*Figure 4.4: Depression graph*

An important sign of well-being is that more days are measured as neutral or higher, than lower. That is, on a scale of 1–10, more days are measured at 5–10 rather than 1–4, and on a scale of 0–20, more days are measured at 10 or above.

# PART 2

## TOOLS IN ENERGY ACCOUNTING

The Energy Accounting method is comprised of partial tools which may be used in different combinations. We consider each strategy of Energy Accounting, or indeed any additional strategy found elsewhere, as part of a 'strategy toolbox' or 'strategy library' that a person can have at their disposal. When seeking to manage stress and improve quality of life, having more tools in your toolbox is very useful as it allows you much more flexibility.

Each individual may find some tools useful and others less so, and for this reason the tools will be described in their own chapters. If you or the person you are working with wish to only use one or two, we again advise personalization of the method over any attempt to use this book as a strict manual.

People may find that during especially stressful or especially calm periods, their use of Energy Accounting is reduced or altered in various ways, and this is okay. The tools provided in this book, as well as the resources we refer to, should be used as needed and as each person feels able to use them at the time. We will address this again in Part 4.

# CHAPTER 5

## The Energy Bank

### WITHDRAWALS AND DEPOSITS

The thinking behind the Energy Bank in Energy Accounting is that all activities have a value in the greater 'budget' of our daily lives. If we simplify it, this means activities can cost energy or give energy. Activities therefore need to be balanced in order to maintain well-being, which sounds simple enough, but creating and maintaining such a balance is, in our view, a complex skill which is learned and refined throughout our lives. Many people learn and refine this skill without really noticing, and some become much better at it than others. However, for those who do not learn 'automatically', a structural concept such as the Energy Bank can be helpful in achieving this balance and learning and internalizing the skills associated with maintaining and monitoring it. Likewise, for those who find themselves overwhelmed due to changes or events, it may be useful for re-examining their situation and how to meet current needs.

The value of these activities – or a person's bank balance or capacity for activities – are different for each person and may even change from day to day or over time, and for that reason, we can only provide examples. We hope they can serve as inspirations in figuring out your own deposits and withdrawals, as well as providing visual and concrete examples of what this process can look like.

It helps to view this concept in the basic terms of deposits and withdrawals. However, we do this knowing that all activities are more complex than merely a single number, especially one that shows only a negative or positive influence on your energy level. For example, an activity like going to a birthday party has a cost in terms of social energy and physical energy, and it involves not only the duration of the event but also who is present, what food is available and how the event is structured (are there games planned, which ones, will there be a sit-down formal meal or buffet of snacks?). It is also a deposit in terms of providing social energy in that it can help to combat loneliness. This will of course depend on social relationships with the other people present.

For an autistic child, such an event may cost a great deal of energy. However, the cost may also be reduced by adjusting details – for example, if the child is allowed to have breaks in a quieter area, is able to bring noise-cancelling headphones or has access to items related to a special interest, the cost may be reduced significantly. Going on public transport may be made easier by having noise-cancelling headphones as well, and for those who are light sensitive, wearing sunglasses all year round is beneficial in reducing the energy cost of travelling.

Deposits may be enhanced by alterations to the activity as well. For example, the quality of time spent on a special interest activity may be enhanced, depending on the person and the interest, by being alone in the room, having an optimal light source, knowing the timeframe of the activity in advance, having snacks and water available, knowing if and when to expect any interruptions, and many other details.

Making small alterations here and there can greatly change the balance of the energy budget, so it is important to pay attention to where beneficial changes can be made, even if these changes do not include a change in the activity or even its duration.

This means that Energy Accounting aims to not only achieve a sense of the value of each activity and event, but also build aware-ness and create a toolbox for the person to decrease the cost of withdrawals and enhance the value of deposits. There may be great differences in what works for each person, which is one of the major reasons we always advocate for personalizing the use of Energy Accounting.

As you will also see, there must be an acknowledgement that starting to use Energy Accounting, figuring out your deposits and withdrawals, as well as the other partial tools, will carry with it a withdrawal of some size/value. Engaging in any change in daily routine will, for a period of time, cost energy. However, the cost should be viewed as an investment. The aim is for the energy spent on learning to use these tools for yourself or for your clients to have a 'return on investment' later, once more awareness is built about how to create an everyday life that works well for you or your clients.

## EXAMPLES OF DEPOSITS AND WITHDRAWALS
Below is a list of examples of deposits and withdrawals. These can perhaps help to begin a conversation about which activities and experiences give and take energy for you or the person you are helping with their Energy Accounting.

It is important to remember that a withdrawal is not necessarily a negative experience. It may be difficult to understand, especially because most withdrawals we think of 'off the top of our heads' tend to be experiences or activities that have a negative impact on both our energy *and* our mood, emotional state or well-being in other ways. However, withdrawals can be activities that are immensely draining on our energy resources, while still being something we look forward to. We have seen examples of this in our clinical work, for example going to a convention or conference to do with an interest, meeting with friends to play tabletop or live action role-playing games, taking an evening class on something the person finds interesting, or travelling somewhere new.

Keep in mind that deposits and withdrawals can change over time in terms of the 'value' of an activity, or they can even change categories depending on how well the person is doing at the time. Because of this, it is important to keep the conversation going.

As mentioned earlier, an activity can be both a deposit and a withdrawal at the same time. This means when you write down a list of deposits and withdrawals, it is okay to place an activity on both sides. Some deposits may also have a 'withdrawal fee', where the activity itself provides a good source of energy, but getting started is difficult for whatever reason.

There are several ways to divide deposits and withdrawals into categories which may be meaningful or make them easier to work with. Here, we attempt to first provide an easy overview of the categories provided. However, another way to view them which may be highly important in the exploration phase of Energy Accounting is to recognize which deposits and withdrawals have long-term effects and which are shorter term. This is especially true when discussing or exploring stress factors. We do this by dividing into categories of basic conditions, primary factors and situational factors. The first two categories may be similar or even overlap to the extent that they do not feel meaningful to some people. However, our choice of dividing them has to do with how we view people with difficulties, mental illness, neurological differences, and so on. Often, people who live with such factors may be referred to as 'stress vulnerable'. Our view is instead that the basic conditions that affect them in their day-to-day lives, such as sensory processing differences or chronic pain, mean that they are subjected to more stressors than others. It may appear to the outside world that they cannot 'handle very much', but in reality, they are handling and overcoming quite a lot every day. By choosing to include such factors in a category of basic conditions rather than merely adjusting their baseline stress threshold to be lower than the average, we seek to recognize their strength and resilience in coping with these daily factors.

| Deposits<br>(Some deposits may fit into several categories. This list of examples should be considered far from comprehensive) | Withdrawals<br>(Some withdrawals may fit into several categories. This list of examples should be considered far from comprehensive) |
|---|---|
| • Social<br>  – Caring for others<br>  – Certain people<br>• Sensory<br>  – Favourite food<br>  – Stimming<br>  – Rhythmical and relaxing sensory experiences<br>• Cognitive<br>  – Meditation/mindfulness<br>  – Animals and nature<br>  – Reading<br>  – Special interest<br>  – Solitude<br>  – Computer games<br>• Physical<br>  – Sleep<br>  – Exercise/physical activity<br>  – Nutrition<br>• Personality traits<br>  – Optimistic<br>  – Cheerful<br>  – Rational<br>  – Tolerant<br>• Moods<br>  – Happy<br>  – Loving<br>  – Calm | • Social<br>  – Socializing<br>  – Being teased or excluded<br>  – Sensitivity to other people's moods<br>  – Certain people<br>• Sensory<br>  – Sensory sensitivity<br>• Cognitive<br>  – Over-analysing social performance<br>  – Perceived injustice<br>  – Too many choices<br>  – Uncertainty (ties into anxiety)<br>  – Change<br>  – Making a mistake<br>  – Daily living skills<br>  – Government agencies<br>  – Body image/perception<br>  – Racing thoughts and rumination<br>  – Being overwhelmed by cognitive input, such as in intense learning environments or exams<br>  – New experiences<br>• Physical<br>  – Illness<br>  – Pain<br>• Personality traits<br>  – Pessimism<br>  – Perfectionism<br>• Moods<br>  – Sadness<br>  – Anger<br>  – Hopelessness<br>• Co-morbidities/Co-existing diagnoses (e.g. Tourette's, PTSD/complex PTSD, obsessive compulsive disorder)<br>  – Symptoms of co-morbid disorders<br>  – Coping with anxiety<br>  – Alexithymia<br>  – Interoception |

*Examples and description of categories/types of factors*

| Basic conditions | Primary factors | Situational factors |
|---|---|---|
| Factors that are long-term/lifelong conditions, affecting daily life, and which may not be expected to disappear completely, though some may be managed and thus their cost lowered | Long-term factors lasting anywhere from a month to several years. They can be changed or even removed completely provided changes are made to the person's life situation | Factors that are relevant only for a short time. They may repeat often, and may be tied to basic conditions, but need not be |
| • Sensory processing differences<br>• Generalized anxiety<br>• Chronic fatigue<br>• Chronic pain<br>• Rumination<br>• Trauma | • Moving<br>• Family separation/ divorce<br>• Coping with a break-up<br>• New job/school<br>• Economic worries<br>• Sleep problems<br>• Exam worries/ stress<br>• Being overworked/ too many tasks/ unmanageable tasks | • Headache<br>• Noise<br>• Sensory sensitivities being triggered<br>• Arguing with someone<br>• Changes to plans<br>• Perceived injustice or disappointment<br>• Overwhelming social events<br>• Acute problems<br>• Oversleeping/being late |

Furthermore, it is important to recognize that, in some cases, a withdrawal can be both a continuous factor as well as a symptom of stress. Sleep problems are a classic example of this. Sleep difficulties are common in autistic people as well as people with chronic or acute anxiety disorders. In many cases, it may be difficult to know whether the sleep problems were a pre-existing constitutional problem, but even if they were, it may still be exacerbated by stress and, in turn, make the stress worse due to the load it places on the body's various systems. Sleep problems can thus become a self-perpetuating cycle.

## DEPOSITS (IN DEPTH)

In the following sections, you will find suggestions for value ranges for each example of an energy deposit. Note that these numbers are based on our experience working with autistic people and may not apply to you. You are not expected to use these numbers or even utilize them as a starting point for yourself or your clients if you do not want to. However, they are there to serve as inspiration and examples. Each section will include a short explanation for what may cause the value range – again, based on our work with autistic people.

## Solitude

Solitude is one of the most effective deposits for most autistic people, as, in most cases, it removes the difficulties of autism by removing the cognitive exhaustion from processing social information and the primary source of interpersonal conflicts. When alone, the mind is not continuously stressed by the presence and interruptions of others, their expectations, judgement, or one's own perception of these. Usually, the result is that other activities deposit more energy than otherwise, or, if the activity is a withdrawal, it withdraws less.

However, solitude as a restorative activity requires time. It is not a matter of being alone for a few minutes – though this can be a useful tool in some cases. In order for solitude to work well for most people, in our clinical experience, it should be relatively extended periods of time, taking into account the person's age and situation. It may require some experimentation to find out what is optimal. Many people who enjoy solitude see benefit from even half an hour or an hour, but there are also some who do not feel truly recharged unless they can have several hours or even a day or days to themselves from time to time.

There are two things to be especially mindful of when it comes to using solitude as a deposit. The first is that too much solitude often leads to not getting enough oxytocin, which impacts feedback inhibition, and also may lead to loneliness; additionally, other people in the person's life may feel rejected, which can cause its own set of interpersonal challenges. The second is that solitude tends to work very poorly if the person fears interruption, and in fact, if there are too many interruptions, the benefits of solitude may be entirely overshadowed.

*Value range 40–100*. At the lower end, it may be just an hour of alone time, knowing that the social activity must be rejoined after this. The higher end would be having extended periods of time, without interruptions, and for some people, knowing how they will be informed if someone is coming to interrupt them may be helpful as well. This could be something as relatively simple as being sent a text 30 minutes before someone comes home.

## Special interest

Engaging in a special interest can provide a calm or refuge in the storm in almost any situation, as long as it is possible to properly engage in the interest. It can create a distraction from some sensory sensitivities, and often, speaking about the special interest will make social interaction less of a withdrawal. When needing a large deposit of energy, time with the special interest in solitude is recommended. On its own, the special interest is often a quicker deposit than solitude, as it is a direct pathway to a positive state of being; however, when the two are combined, this is often the absolute quickest way to restore balance to the account.

It can also be used as a thought blocker in the sense that it can distract from negative and intrusive thoughts better than most other activities. However, in much the same way as solitude, the value of time spent on a special interest is very dependent on the circumstances. If there are interruptions, the value can be greatly decreased. It is also important to remember that the negative thoughts have been suppressed and not resolved, for example when the computer is switched off, there is a deluge of compressed negative thoughts to cope with. The contrast between the two states of mind can be difficult to cope with.

*Value range 40–100*. Someone may rate their time with a special interest at 40 if they felt rushed, if they did not have proper access to the interest, or if they were feeling watched or evaluated in a negative way. They may rate it much higher if they have access under circumstances in which they feel very comfortable, there is an appropriate length of time and they have the things necessary to engage with and enjoy the activity.

## Physical activity

Many autistic people are not fans of exercise, either because the sensation of sweating feels unpleasant to them, or because they have poor coordination or proprioception and have been teased for their coordination and agility. However, physical activity does not necessarily have to be team sports or running, jumping, climbing or going to the gym. It can be a walk in nature, or playing a mobile or console game that requires movement, or swimming or gardening. The importance of physical activity cannot be overstated, as it increases the health of the entire body, including the brain. Many people are able to notice the difference in how much energy they feel they have during periods where they exercise regularly, and during those times when they are more sedentary. Others may not notice themselves, but those around them are likely to see the effects. It is important to be creative in coming up with the right type of activity that suits body type, personality, and any relevant disabilities or handicaps, taking into account that not everyone is able-bodied. A personal trainer or a physiotherapist may provide guidance in what physical activities would be appropriate for particular body types, personalities and past experiences of physical exercise. Sometimes, it is possible to combine physical exercise with the special interest, with solitude, or both.

As a deposit, physical activity is tricky to set a value range on, as people may not feel at the time that it is a deposit – in fact sometimes, it may feel very much like a withdrawal. However, due to its contributions to overall physical and mental health, we consider it a deposit on the bottom line.

*Value range 10–50.* Value ranges will depend highly on the person, and how inclined they are towards the particular activity. Values may also likely increase when combined with an interest (not necessarily the primary interest), with socializing with friends, or with a pet (e.g. walking the dog).

## Animals and nature

Being in nature is generally beneficial for humans, and there are countless studies showing these benefits, for example in cognition and mood, across age groups. Many autistic people have immense benefit from spending time with animals or being in nature. Being in the garden, taking a walk in the forest or park (though not at times when it is filled with people) or going to the beach can all be good ideas, though there are many more. When it comes to animals, most people think of dogs and cats as the first options, but so many autistic people also have a wonderful connection with other animals such as horses, rodents, reptiles and insects. It may be, in fact, that the best thing for the mental health of someone is to have a turtle, tarantula or snake.

Tony saw a 14-year-old autistic adolescent who was experiencing severe depression. He visibly lacked energy and connection to his family and peers. His physical posture was 'closed' and he was reluctant to engage in conversation with anyone. Tony noted in the referral letter that he had an interest in snakes and asked the adolescent to choose his favourite species of snake and why he made that choice to initiate a conversation and engagement. The adolescent's response was instantaneous and in complete contrast to his previous mental state. He became excited and animated, describing the qualities of the different snake species, and he engaged in a reciprocal and energized conversation. There were no signs of social withdrawal and depression. During the conversation on snakes, he momentarily became morose when he explained that his mother hated snakes and forbade him from having a snake as a pet. Tony turned to his mother and said that having a pet snake would be a significant part of his treatment of depression, and reluctantly she agreed he could have a snake. At the next appointment a month later, there were no signs of depression and he seemed very happy. When Tony asked why his mood had improved, he replied enthusiastically, 'I have two snakes now!'

*Value range 20–80.* Because these activities are so highly depend-ent on individual enjoyment, we do see people rate them at very different ranges. People who have anxiety regarding going outside do, of course, have a much harder time with it than those who enjoy it outright, and we acknowledge that this does not feel like a deposit for everyone.

Low deposit values may be the result of not being particularly interested in nature or animals, or perhaps it being not very good weather for a walk outside. Higher numbers are likely to happen for those who have intrinsic enjoyment of nature and animals, but for animal lovers, meeting a nice dog while on a walk can, by itself, be a deposit of perhaps 50 or 60.

### Computer games

Computer and console games provide a visual distraction as well as entertainment and can differ vastly in difficulty, which means this deposit consists of being challenged and succeeding, or relaxing with games. Many games can be played alone, which can ease the stress level quite a lot. Even games that do have social components can be significantly less stressful than other social interaction, because the social aspects are contextually bound to the game. There is no need to read facial expressions and body language or engage in 'small talk'. The social rules of the game are simple, clear and consistent, with text or voice communication often revolving around the game. This can be true to some extent even if gaming with a friend takes place in the same room, as there is the benefit of parallel rather than face-to-face activity which is often easier and less stressful for people who find social interaction and reading non-verbal communication difficult.

It is important with games to keep in mind that they may become addictive. Many modern games are designed to keep people playing for as long as possible, or to keep people coming back to the game every so often throughout the day and purchasing components to the game. This can become a problem which leads to a meltdown if access to the game is then impossible for whatever reason. A set of rules for when and how long the game can be accessed, and under which circumstances, may help with this and reduce stress and uncertainty. For example, if a child knows in advance that they are not allowed to play the game during a birthday dinner, and they have been provided with information about what is expected, this can make things easier. Note that the addictiveness of games does not apply only to children, nor to people who find social interaction challenging. Games are designed to be addictive to all people, and they affect everyone's brains, just as social media does. App-based games are no exception, either.

This is not to say that games cannot have great benefits, however, and we are not in any way discouraging the use of these games as a deposit. We are only suggesting some caution in the way in which this deposit is used in daily life.

Access to computer, console or app-based games should be adjusted depending on the person's age, and the current conditions of their life.

*Value range 10–50.* Lower value ranges tend to be associated with those who play to fill their time, or to distract from negative thoughts and emotions. Higher value ranges tend to be when people play with genuine enjoyment and interest, and find success within the game.

## Meditation

Our colleague, Michelle Garnett, a clinical psychologist, has been incorporating yoga in her practice with autistic adolescents and adults for over ten years. She embraced yoga for many reasons, especially the philosophy of yoga that accepts the person as they are and helps them find their true self and subsequent self-acceptance and a sense of well-being. The benefits of mediating include being in the present moment, and being more aware of the body (i.e. living less in one's head). When suffering is experienced, the philosophy of yoga teaches that we should notice the experience and move in closer to observe what is happening with love and compassion. Suffering is a natural part of human experience that comes and goes. With intense anxiety, depression or anger or when experiencing painful sensory experiences, the practice of yoga says lovingly, 'Stay, observe what is happening and label the experience. The experience does not define you.

Notice the thought, emotion or sensation and what is happening in your body. Notice if there is any way that you can bring a sense of ease into your experience.' Yoga can bring a sense of calming and the foundation of meaningful relationships.

A review of the research studies on meditation as a potential therapy for autistic people has confirmed that meditation not only brings relief for many of the challenges of autistic individuals but also improves the quality of their family and social life (Sequeira & Ahmed 2012).

*Value range 50–90.*

Note, these values are for those who benefit from meditation. Others may not feel a benefit, and their value range will reflect that.

## Caring for others

A great way to increase the bonding and well-being hormone oxytocin is by caring and doing good things for others. It may seem counterintuitive that by giving you are receiving, but this is why being kind to others can feel enjoyable. When we see others respond positively to our behaviour, our nervous system rewards us. It is a rather smart encouragement mechanism and energy deposit, if we think about it from an evolutionary perspective. Humans survive better when they are together, and so our brains and nervous systems make us feel good about creating social bonds.

People often feel a great emotional benefit from being kind to others, either by helping them with a task, or providing care in some way. They feel valued and appreciated. This care may not be expressed in a traditional sense, and may not always include overt social interaction. Providing help with a specific task, especially if this is related to an interest or a skill the person has, may be especially restorative. There is both the inherent sense of having helped someone and being valued, and having used a skill or knowledge well and solved a problem. Likewise, caring for animals can be a good energy restorative. Many people also feel great benefit from volunteering in a capacity which they find meaningful. Aside from the bonding aspect, there is also the feeling of accomplishment, and having contributed to the well-being of someone else.

*Value range 10–50.*

Note, these values are for those who benefit from meditation. Others may not feel a benefit, and their value range will reflect that.

*Value range 10–50.*

## Nutrition

Quite like physical activity, nutrition is a deposit to the account that works to stabilize our nervous systems, and because it does the important work 'in the background' so to speak, many forget to recognize it as a part of the balance of accounts. Certain dishes which are favourite foods may be a more direct, noticeable deposit. Some people do find certain foods to be unappealing, and being made to eat these, or even smelling them, may be an energy withdrawal. Someone may not like a certain type of food either due to taste, colour or texture, and may see it as a chore to eat. This can sometimes be helped by cooking in a particular manner, by adding other flavours, mixing with other food items, or changing the texture by boiling, searing or even blending. Sometimes, it can be hard to find alternatives – luckily, the internet is a marvellous library of recipes and ideas.

When specific food items cause an acute energy withdrawal, remembering the stabilizing work they do, in terms of providing body and brain with required nutrients, can help. A diet which is too rich in, for example, sugar can not only cause illnesses such as diabetes, but will also influence daily fluctuations in mood and energy, creating sudden feelings of exhaustion throughout the day, prompting people to consume yet more sugar (or caffeine).

A general, varied diet, avoiding sugar and junk food, seems to provide an overall boost to acute mood and mood stability, which contributes to stabilizing the stress threshold as well.

*Value range 10–60.*

## Sleep

The rest achieved for the body and brain during sleep is one of the most crucial energy deposits available. However, over 60 per cent of autistic adults complain about sleep problems, autistic women being more likely than autistic men to have poor sleep quality (Jovevska *et al.* 2020). These include trouble falling asleep, the quality and depth of sleep and the duration of sleep. Insomnia is considered a common co-morbidity of autism. Research confirms that those autistic children and adults who have sleep problems are more likely to have higher levels of stress, anxiety, depression and fatigue (Mazurek & Sohl 2016; Stewart *et al.* 2020). On average, autistic adults sleep for up to an hour less each night than typical age peers due to later bedtimes, difficulty falling asleep and earlier waking. Difficulty falling asleep can be due to several characteristics associated with autism, including sensory sensitivity, lack of daylight during the day and aspects of impaired interoception and cognitively not perceiving the internal signals of tiredness. Another characteristic is racing thoughts that have been suppressed by distracting activities such as playing a computer game and electronic media. This strategy affects sleep onset in terms of racing thoughts and emotions returning when the computer game is switched off and there is the thought 'void' when the light is switched off at bedtime.

This can be so troublesome that it can be tempting to turn to sleeping aids of various forms, such as medications which cause tiredness, or alcohol. We do not recommend these, especially as they often impact the quality of sleep, even if falling asleep becomes easier.

Sleep is a time to cognitively and emotionally process and store thoughts, memories and feelings. It is a neurological 'defrag'. Rest and sleep are vital energy restoratives, both in terms of physical health and mental health. Not getting enough sleep, or getting bad sleep, can mean this category is greatly diminished as an energy deposit, and can even subjectively feel like a withdrawal, so it is important to prioritize sleep when creating a schedule, and if the person is not sleeping well, to examine ways to improve sleep. These include the use of the natural medicine melatonin to assist in falling asleep, reviewing sensory experiences that can keep you awake, having a consistent bedtime and pre-sleep routine, no adrenaline- or dopamine-releasing screen time an hour before bedtime, avoiding consuming above recommended levels of alcohol or taking illegal mood-altering substances in the evening, and learning relaxation and mindfulness activities. Other ways to facilitate falling asleep include avoiding sugar and caffeine for the last hour or two before bedtime, reading a book or magazine or listening to an audiobook or calming music to lower the heart rate, making the environment relaxing and reviewing positive experiences of the day rather than ruminating on stressful events. If these strategies are not successful, it may be worth considering a referral to a hospital sleep clinic for further investigation of sleep difficulties and the development of a treatment plan for improved sleep.

*Value range 10–100.* Sleep is one of the hardest activities to rate, as it spans from very poor sleep, to high-quality sleep that leaves you feeling rested and recharged.

## *Reading*
This category may differ greatly for some individuals, but for many, reading is a joy. Fiction series in particular can become a good deposit of energy. Fiction transports us away from reality and distracts from any aspects of it that may be worrying or otherwise causing distress. It also provides a safe place to explore the inner worlds of other people, emotions and social interactions, through the descriptions of characters. Reading can provide access to knowledge about special interests such as science fiction, as well as about the world in general. It can give a sense of putting the world into systems, understanding things better, which can ease anxiety or even create feelings of joy. Reading non-fiction can, for some, create a sense of grounding, something that feels concrete and easy. Accumulating facts and information can be soothing and an energy deposit, and by knowing these things, it can create a sense of self-identity.

*Value range 10–80.* The lower value range may apply to situations in which it is harder to focus, whereas higher values likely apply only for those who find great pleasure in reading, and in situations when they have access to reading topics or genres they enjoy the most and can focus on them.

## Favourite food

Most people have favourite foods. They are associated with happy memories, events, or perhaps they are just extra tasty. Whatever it is, having these foods gives a little extra boost, and can help restore or keep up energy – of course, this does not mean they can repair a meltdown, though this can be true for some.

Importantly, favourite foods are not always healthy and thus must be consumed in moderation. This is an energy tool that is useful only when it works in balance with a healthy eating habit. This is the reason we have kept it as a separate point from nutrition. Favourite foods as a deposit work less effectively if used too often, as well. Think of it as having dessert – if you have dessert every day, it becomes less special, and even expected. Once it is an expected part of life, it is a negative thing to not have it on any particular day. Basically, be careful not to overdo it.

*Value range 20–50.*

## Stimming and soothing behaviour

Stimming refers to repetitive actions, mannerisms and often movements or vocalizing, which create a particular sensory experience. These often function as soothing behaviours that are used when the person is stressed or anxious, but they can also be expressive of positive emotions, or they can create positive sensory experiences. Examples are hand flapping, rocking and humming, but it should be noted that there are many variations of stimming out there, and it can be argued that many fidgety behaviours such as clicking a pen or tapping your foot could fall into the category too – these are perhaps merely more conventional, and therefore often socially accepted, variations.

Stimming or sensory experiences can be a way for people to create sensory input for themselves, often to block overwhelming sensory input coming from other sources. The actions are mesmerizing and create a sense of detachment from sensory or social experiences.

Some autistic people stim automatically when they feel the need; however, many can learn to use stimming as a conscious tool to alleviate the effects of feeling stressed, an unpleasant sensory experience, or to create a positive experience to restore energy. Also, it does not need to be the same stims as the person uses when feeling overwhelmed. There are many sensory toys available online, such as tangles or fidget spinners.

Stimming can make others stare at you if you are in a public setting, and while many people may not care about being looked at, others feel embarrassed or exposed. For those who feel negatively impacted by the attention of others while stimming, our experience is that there are two ways to lessen the negative impact. One is to have some pre-scripted ways to inform a person that the action helps you to relax or concentrate. The script may or may not include information about autism or other relevant diagnoses, according to personal preferences. The other is, if the person likes the idea and is able, to learn secondary stimming behaviours which are more subtle or easily hidden in public. Often, these take a while to feel automatic, and they may never feel as effective as their natural stimming behaviour. However, if the new behaviour helps to alleviate the stressor of feeling badly about others looking, the removal or alleviation of that stressor means it can still be preferable in certain situations. We would like to emphasize that we would never encourage someone to stop stimming for the sake of appearing less autistic. These points are solely to do with the autistic person's comfort in a given situation.

Note that people who have a higher tendency to mask unconventional behaviours may have trained themselves to not stim, even in situations when this would be helpful. Indeed, there may be an internalized rule to not do these things as they may cause others to perceive you as odd. However, despite this it can be beneficial for some to relearn how to stim, as the emotional regulation it can create will still function as a stress relief mechanism. During the period of relearning to stim, it can initially feel awkward, and may be a less effective deposit.

*Value range 10–40.*


## WITHDRAWALS (IN DEPTH)
### Socializing
Social interaction often causes the primary amount of energy withdrawals in a day for autistic people, introverts and others who find socializing challenging, either directly or indirectly. Socializing itself is incredibly draining, even though it can also be rewarding in other ways. Keep in mind that the amount of energy spent on socializing can depend not only on the timeframe and physical surroundings, but also on how defined the interaction is (are specific activities planned, and are these activities fun and pleasant or unwanted and stressful?) and with whom the interaction takes place. Furthermore, everyone can have a preference for being around certain people and can be more or less challenged by interacting with others, depending on personalities, shared interests and many other factors.

Many people can relate to the experience that some people are, in astronomical psychology terms, 'black holes' for energy, such that one feels drained after socializing with them even for short periods, whereas others radiate energy like the sun, causing one to feel energized. For autistic people, the same is true, except the draining aspects of socializing – consciously analysing everything, cognitive overload, and so on – often overpower any energy that may otherwise be restored. However, there can still be a very clear sense of having had positive social interactions or not, and the positive ones can be very important in combating feelings of loneliness.

It is important to note that the need for solitude after having a social interaction is not a rejection of other people. For those who find socializing challenging, it tends to be a withdrawal no matter whom they spend time with. This means you can be their best friend, genuinely the most relaxing person for them to be around, and they may have genuine and lifelong affection for you, but they still need solitude to recharge. This is often a challenge to explain to significant others as well as close family members as they may have difficulties in not perceiving the need for solitude as a rejection. *Value range 20–80.*

---

### *Phrases to explain to others that socializing is an energy withdrawal*

My brain works differently. I spend a lot of energy analysing what is happening in social situations because it does not happen automatically for me. It is not intuitive for me. This means socializing does not recharge me the way it does for many others.

I am the sort of person who notices a lot of details that others might not, things that seem insignificant sometimes, and this can make it hard to focus on things that matter, such as a conversation I am having. Even though the conversation is interesting, this still happens, so I spend loads of energy on trying to focus on the things I need to. This means that even though I know you really well and enjoy spending time with you, I still need to spend time alone to recharge.

I am the sort of person who needs alone-time to recharge. It has nothing to do with any specific people. It is not that I want to get away from anyone specifically, but rather that I need some alone-time. When I get that alone-time I am then able to enjoy the subsequent social time I engage in.

## Over-analysing social performance

While this also occurs during an interaction, there is usually a period of time either very soon after the interaction, or possibly when trying to fall asleep at night, when social performance analysis begins again. This is when details of the interaction are analysed in depth and, in spite of this, are often not truly resolved. Even where nothing went wrong, there can still be over-analysis of social performance.

Because the analysis often does not resolve, this tendency can cause tremendous problems with falling asleep, as well as with attempting to relax without an activity to occupy or block the social analysis – such as reading or screen time. Any time that the mind is not occupied by a subject, thinking can quickly turn to analysing and ruminating on recent social interactions, which can then devolve into anxiety. People can get cognitively 'stuck' on this thinking track, conducting a social 'autopsy' for hours at a time if they do not know how to 'change tracks' so to speak, stop themselves, and do something else.

*Value range 30–70.*

Generally speaking, the more anxious people become over the analysis, the harder the cycle is to break and the more energy is spent both due to anxiousness and the fight to break the negative spiral of thoughts. For this reason, an important element of lowering the value of this withdrawal is learning to recognize the signs of the spiral beginning, and finding ways to break it early, through distractions, realistic alternative thoughts, or any other strategy that works for that person.

## Racing thoughts

A characteristic associated with autism is to have accelerating thoughts, and it can feel as if these thoughts are like an avalanche or a tsunami in the sense that they build and overwhelm the person, who feels unable to get away. Even when coping mechanisms are learned for how to stop the racing thoughts, energy is still required to apply a cognitive 'brake'. The racing thoughts can also lead to racing speech, which can be confusing to the conversation partner.

Another way to cope with racing thoughts is to engage in a special interest as a thought 'blocker', but again, the racing thoughts and the effort it takes to transition to a new activity mean that an energy withdrawal has happened. With Energy Accounting as well as other approaches, we seek to prevent this withdrawal from being larger, and from taking time away from other activities and thoughts which are more useful and desired by the person.

Aside from the already mentioned analysis of social performance, racing thoughts and rumination are commonly centred around: negative experiences, often going back to childhood, current world events that are concerning to the person, acquired knowledge which the person finds disturbing, or even general worries, for example regarding sensory experiences, school or work performance.

*Value range 30–70.*

### Sensitivity to other people's moods – emotional empathy

This withdrawal shows itself in several different ways. However, before it can be acknowledged, we first need to dispel the myth that autistic people have poor empathy, or even none. The reality, confirmed in autobiographies, clinical experience and research, is that the autistic person can and usually does have empathy but the profile of empathy abilities may be different.

Psychologists conceptualize three components of empathy. The first is *cognitive empathy* – to read someone's non-verbal communication and context to determine what they are feeling. Autism is associated with a difficulty reading subtle non-verbal or context cues that indicate someone's mental state. If those subtle cues are not perceived, then an anticipated empathic response will not be given, which may lead to accusations of a lack of empathy. The second component is *emotional empathy* – the ability to feel an emotion that resonates with the perceived emotional state of another person. A characteristic of autism is when the signs of distress are perceived, to subsequently feel someone's distress to a much greater degree than those who are not autistic. There is often not an absence of internal emotional response, but an amplification. The third component is *behavioural empathy* – to respond in an anticipated way that alleviates the distress. Preferred emotional repair mechanisms for an autistic person may be solitude, distraction and suppression, while a typical person would use and anticipate affection, compassion and attentive listening. When these anticipated responses are not given, the autistic person is again accused of lacking empathy.

A relevant characteristic of autism that we are starting to explore is empathic attunement or a 'sixth sense' ability to perceive and absorb the negative emotions of others, especially disappointment, anxiety and agitation. In effect, this is emotional empathy, but without a filter. The person often lacks the ability to distinguish where the emotion comes from, especially in highly stressful situations. The following quotations from our clinical experience describe intense emotional empathy:

> There's a kind of instant subconscious reaction to the emotional states of other people that I have understood better in myself over the years.

> If someone approaches me for a conversation and they are full of worry, fear or anger, I find myself suddenly in the same state of emotion.

> I am able to distinguish very subtle cues that others would not see, or it might be a feeling I pick up from them.

This means that an autistic child may react very strongly to his mother being sad, without fully understanding why and knowing what to do to alleviate her sadness. An autistic adolescent said, 'Human comfort has always been a mystery.' Several autistic adults explain that their mechanism for knowing how others feel involves being 'infected' by other people's emotions that are 'imported', then registering and sometimes amplifying the emotions within themselves. There can be the cognitive recognition that the emotion does not belong to them due to a personal experience, but has become a source of the emotional 'infection'. We would explain that the emotions seem to be 'mirrored' and absorbed before being cognitively processed and that processing them can be overwhelming and exhausting. This means being vulnerable to someone else's emotions in social situations and can be one of the reasons to avoid social situations as a form of emotional protection.

Once the emotion is recognized and processed, the autistic person is likely to spend energy trying to repair the negative emotion of the other person and themselves and on thinking through options and reactions, feeling anxious in trying to avoid making a social and/or emotional mistake and upsetting the person further, and seeking emotional equilibrium.

It is important to note that another person's negative emotion does not have to relate to the autistic person in order for the emotion to drain energy from them. One of the first cases in which Energy Accounting was used clinically revealed that a young girl was greatly affected by her mother's emotions, even if the mother was upset about something completely unrelated.

*Value range 20–80.*

## Misinterpreting intentions

Autism is often associated with a difficulty reading non-verbal communication which often expresses someone's emotions, thoughts and intentions. There can be a difficulty accurately reading someone's emotional state when the non-verbal communication is perceived as ambiguous or too fleeting to cognitively process, or indeed, if there is too much information to process at once, for example during a party, or while in a public setting. Research has indicated that an autistic person is more likely to attribute an ambiguous face as expressing anger and to have difficulty determining if a particular act was accidental or deliberate, sometimes assuming malicious intent when this was not intended. This can lead to potential conflict and increased stress and energy depletion.

*Value range 20–80.* Often, the value assigned to this sensitivity is determined by the moods the person perceives on that day. This means milder or positive emotions may be entirely neutral, a mild withdrawal, or even on some occasions a small deposit. However, more extreme emotions and especially negative emotions may be overwhelming and the withdrawal will be more extreme as well, potentially contributing to depression and greater difficulties with mood regulation.

## Alexithymia

Alexithymia is a psychological term to describe a difficulty converting thoughts and feelings into speech. Alexithymia is associated with, but not exclusive to, autism, and not every autistic person has alexithymia. However, for those who do have alexithymia, there can be a difficulty determining exactly which emotion is being experienced, and in precisely and accurately describing the emotion and degree of expression using speech. When asked 'What are you feeling now?', the answer may be 'I don't know', which is not being obtuse or evasive. The complete version of this answer may be: 'I don't know how to grasp one of the many intangible thoughts and feelings swirling in my mind, and then to explain those thoughts and feelings in words that you will understand.' An autistic adult explained that, initially, all her milder negative emotions are described by the term 'ick'. She knows it is not a nice feeling but is unsure if she is feeling anxious, angry or sad, so they are all 'ick'. As the feelings become more intense, she is then able to cognitively rather than intuitively determine the emotional dimension, strength of the emotion and words that precisely describe the intensity. Most people can accurately and eloquently describe their subtle inner world of thoughts and emotions, but this ability can be elusive for those who have alexithymia. If there is a difficulty determining and describing feelings, there will be a difficulty managing feelings from a personal and support person's perspective. A difficulty communicating thoughts and feelings in a conversation or psychotherapy can contribute to greater emotional confusion and decrease the effectiveness of 'talk' therapy. However, our experience has been that emotions can be identified and communicated by developing abilities in the arts, for example expressing the inner world of emotions and thoughts in a drawing, choosing or composing music, poetry and prose, and dance. Some autistic people have used these means of expression to achieve a successful career in the arts.

*Value range 10–50.* As a basic condition of a person's life, alexithymia may represent a more or less constant withdrawal of, say, 10–30 energy every day. However, in situations where there is an acute need to communicate about one's emotional state, the frustration of having such difficulties may result in a higher energy withdrawal.

## Being teased or rejected

Unfortunately, many autistic people are teased, rejected, humiliated or bullied. This is a major cause of psychological distress and considerable energy withdrawals, due to both the events themselves and to rumination, sometimes for decades after the event, trying to figure out the motives of the participants, what could have been done differently, and so on. There may be exhausting racing thoughts and rumination about specific events, which can cause difficulties in falling asleep, and the anticipation of these experiences increases anxiety.

Being teased can also have a negative effect on mood even when it is not intended as mean. What is perceived by others as friendly banter or jokes can be misinterpreted as malicious and require the expenditure of considerable mental energy to determine whether the words and actions were friendly or designed to cause distress, leading to ruminating on the intention of a 'friendly' experience. This can also lead to problems with falling asleep, which can create other issues. However, we recognize that when bullying is involved, there can be additional problems with a single traumatic experience, or cumulative bullying that leads to signs of PTSD with, for example, flashbacks and reoccurring nightmares. This may be better dealt with in trauma therapy.

Note that bullying, especially over long periods of time, can be a triggering or exacerbating factor in the development of anxiety disorders, depression and other mental illnesses. This means that aside from each single event being highly uncomfortable or even frightening to the person, there are long-term mental health consequences. This also means that while bullying can be a situational factor in energy withdrawal, it may also be a primary factor – something that is ongoing but which can be made worse by, for example, moving schools or changing employment – and the resulting withdrawals can constitute a basic condition for that person for years or even decades.

*Value range 60–100*. It is possible there would be lower values for small misunderstandings, but for the most part, we see that those who are bullied and rejected by peers are highly affected, both in the situation and in general in their daily lives.

## Changes

Adjusting to changes does not come naturally or easily to an autistic person. The first reaction is often one of anxiety, insecurity and, potentially, refusal. Internally, the feeling of plans changing is unpleasant at best, and can even feel chaotic. The ability to cope with changes and unexpected events can improve with age, and, certainly, having spare energy 'credit' in the account will help. However, young children, who have not achieved the degree of cognitive maturity to accommodate changes, can respond with a meltdown.

Changes are not set events in terms of the amount of energy withdrawal, however. The circumstances under which a change happens can be important, as can previous knowledge or estimation of how likely a change was. Being made aware of a change of plans before leaving the house may be far less costly in terms of energy. Likewise, being made aware the day before rather than in the morning provides more time to process new plans and adjust. The activity being changed or cancelled also matters to the individual.

A child may look forward to seeing their friend, but on arrival it turns out that there is another child visiting as well and this child is not a friend. The energy and emotional cost of this may ruin the entire day. Being informed the evening before would perhaps still result in a meltdown, but to a lesser degree, and they may be more receptive to suggestions for three children playing together rather than the anticipated two children.

An adult going to a meeting at work in the afternoon and finding out on arrival that it has been cancelled may spend hours adjusting to the change in their expectations and schedule, losing effective time at work. However, if they had been informed on arrival at the office that morning, it may have given them time to rearrange their day without too much additional hassle.

These two short examples show the vast differences in factors affecting the energy cost of change, and serve to demonstrate that changes are not only unpredictable in life, but also in the value range in Energy Accounting. The subject of adjusting to change will be handled in more depth later in the book.

One source of energy depletion related to change is transitions, even a transition to a preferred activity. The energy is consumed by having to 'close down' the mental plan for the previous activity and 'start up' a new mental plan.

*Value range 10–80.* Smaller or more insignificant changes may have a much lower value as a withdrawal than larger changes, which can result in heightened levels of anxiousness or even an immediate meltdown.

### Making a mistake
The perception of having made a mistake, whether at school or college, in a social context or at work, can lead to anxious thoughts, rumination, feelings of shame and self-criticism. As

such, making a mistake will carry a cost to the energy budget. As with changes, mistakes are the sort of withdrawal that may trigger a meltdown.

However, it is often not whether a mistake has been made that is important, but whether the person themselves *believes* that they have made a mistake. For this reason, if they believe they have made a social mistake, for example, others reassuring them that this is not the case may still not alleviate the anxiety entirely. If the reaction of others is to confirm that a mistake was made, this will add significantly to the energy cost, as this may combine the event with teasing, bullying or sarcasm, or with the feeling of being unwanted, rejected and not good enough.

Due to a tendency towards perfectionism combined with lower fine motor skills, autistic children and adolescents may have an especially difficult time making mistakes while writing or drawing. Dysgraphia is associated with autism. This can be in the early school years or it can persist into adulthood. These 'mistakes' often lead to erasing and rewriting or drawing many times and this can lead to a meltdown, especially if other people do not react with understanding and know how to calm the person. The cost of making a mistake can be significant in the moment, but can also be spread out over several timeframes during the day or week if the person also ruminates on their mistake later or there seem to be more than the usual number of mistakes or failures in the day. Therefore, teaching the person how to cope with making mistakes and working on their self-acceptance and self-worth is highly beneficial in the long run.

*Value range 20–100.* Lower value ranges may be associated with smaller mistakes or imperfections, whereas the higher values are likely to be associated with situations in which the mistake has larger consequences, is pointed out by others, or the person feels as though others are looking at and evaluating them. For example, if you are late or drop something, it can feel more embarrassing if you think or feel that others are looking at you. Note that autistic people and introverted or socially anxious people are less likely to actually look at others to check whether or not their perception of being watched is true.

## Sensory sensitivity

Each autistic person, and person with sensory processing differences, has their own profile of sensory sensitivities, some more pronounced and debilitating than others. Coping with and compensating for these on a daily basis, which is energy depleting, can make people with sensory sensitivities vulnerable to developing stress, and can even trigger acute distress, panic, a meltdown or shutdown.

Because each expression of sensory sensitivity is so different both in form and intensity, so is the withdrawal cost. This means that in order to understand the daily energy budget, it is important to have a good understanding of which sensory sensitivities are relevant to that person's daily life, including the ones that may not occur frequently, but which trigger acute distress for them.

Sensory sensitivities may also change during the person's lifetime, which can cause some confusion. Things that used to be unbearable can become somewhat tolerable, and things that were once acceptable or manageable are suddenly overwhelming. Likewise, sensory sensitivities may differ in energy cost depending on circumstances and general stress level.

A sensory sensitivity can affect all sensory systems and can be present from infancy to old age. An auditory sensitivity can be for unanticipated 'sharp' noises such as a dog barking, a specific pitch, like a hairdryer or vacuum cleaner, or volume such as someone shouting, or other auditory experiences that are subjectively unbearable, such as someone singing off key. The degree of auditory perception can be extraordinary such that people with sensory processing differences can actually hear the noise from a fluorescent light bulb or the wifi and may not be able to distract themselves from that sound.

Visual sensitivity can be for types of illumination such as fluorescent lights and bright sunlight or not being able to tolerate the flickering or brightness of a computer screen. We have experience with clients who have their screens always set to night mode or dark mode, so that the light is softer to the eyes. Some people have a clear perception of dust particles in the air or find some colour combinations too intense and aversive. There may also be synesthesia involved, which is when one sensory experience is processed as another, such as hearing colours or tasting a tactile experience. Tactile sensitivity can include hypersensitivity leading to not tolerating labels and seams in clothing and avoiding greetings that involve a handshake, kiss or hug. Olfactory sensitivity can include feeling nauseous when perceiving someone's deodorant or perfume. People with sensory processing differences are likely to experience aversive sensory sensations almost every day, some predictable, others a surprise, which can lead to a state of constant vigilance and anxiety that can significantly deplete energy.

*Value range 10–70.* The lower values tend to be sensory sensitivities that are relatively mild, and in situations where the person has the capacity to cope with it. The higher values are often associated with sensory sensitivities which are triggered suddenly or to an extreme.

## Daily living skills
Brushing one's teeth, showering, shopping, cooking, tidying, cleaning dishes and doing laundry are examples of everyday activities that most people simply go through, not giving them much thought beyond 'this needs doing'. However, for an autistic person or someone with impaired executive functioning, these are not simple activities. Something like showering involves many tasks or components, all of which must be completed, some in a specific order – like shampooing before conditioning one's hair. Autistic people and others with challenges in executive functioning are often continuously aware of all of these tasks, and spend cognitive resources keeping track of the sequence and where they are in the sequence. For many autistic people, there is a sense of worry that elements may be forgotten, or that the sheer number of daily living activities that need to be completed is overwhelming.

A reason for this is often challenges or impairments in executive functioning which govern the planning, prioritizing and organization of resources needed for the tasks, the initiation of the tasks, switching between tasks, and time management. Many autistic adults find tidying or cleaning difficult – not because they do not know how to do it but because getting a grasp of what needs doing, in what order, and to what level of detail and performance, may get in the way of initiating the task or may overwhelm the person even while they are in the process of completing the task. This means that daily living skills need to be a part of an Energy Accounting schedule.

Around 75 per cent of autistic children and adults have or qualify for an additional diagnosis of an attention deficit disorder, either hyperactive or inattentive, and with this comes an increase in executive function impairments. This means having additional difficulties with, for example, staying focused while doing things like tidying or cleaning. This can come across as being very ineffective but in different ways. Examples that we hear often include: while putting something away, in a drawer or cupboard, realizing the drawer or cupboard needs tidying and starting that project instead of continuing with the original task. Or, while tidying, finding something that needs to go to a different room, and then in that room, finding a new task. An hour later, the person has done a whole lot, but the physical environment may not look very different from when they started. This can be highly discouraging to the person and they may feel that they are not good at tidying or cleaning when, in fact, their issue is staying focused on the task. There can be a perception that medication such as methylphenidate, given to people with attention disorders, fixes this problem entirely, but this is rarely – if ever – the case. Rather than eliminating this issue, it *alleviates* it. Strategies to manage executive function challenges are still highly beneficial even when medication is involved, and medication may make it easier for the person to learn strategies.

*Value range 20–60.* The value range for daily living skills tends to be relatively high. This is because of the often dual challenge of executive function issues and sensory sensitivities. Note that this type of withdrawal tends to happen several times a day.

### Coping with anxiety

Anxiety disorders are incredibly common in autistic people. Over 40 research publications have confirmed that an anxiety disorder is the most common mental health problem for autistic children and adults, with prevalence figures ranging from 11 to 84 per cent, while there is a prevalence of only 5 per cent for the general population (Gotham *et al.* 2015; Hwang *et al.* 2020; Joshi *et al.* 2013; Nimmo-Smith *et al.* 2020). An internet survey of over 300 autistic adults indicated that over 98 per cent ranked anxiety as the greatest cause of stress in their daily lives, greater than the stress associated with making and keeping friendships and relationships, finding and maintaining employment and coping with daily living skills (Attwood *et al.* 2014). Coping with anxiety on a daily basis is a major withdrawal of energy for those who have symptoms of an anxiety disorder such as obsessive compulsive disorder (OCD), generalized anxiety disorder (GAD) and specific phobias (often related to sensory sensitivity, performance anxiety or fear of rejection). Each person is, again, different, and so the particular ways in which anxiety affects the energy budget will be individual. This means that each person's specific anxiety symptoms and their depth must be taken into account, including the severity of these, as well as any possible medication and psychological therapy that may be involved in treatment.

Note that changes in medication affect the symptoms of anxiety (or any other co-morbid disorder that is medicated), and that any changes in side effects that follow may cause changes in the values assigned in the budget. Thus, alterations like these take time to adjust to on the planning level.

*Value range 20–100.* For the lower values, this often means the person experiences mild anxiety or worry, perhaps on a daily level, but does not necessarily qualify for a separate clinical anxiety diagnosis. Higher values often indicate someone who has a separate anxiety disorder diagnosis – or who qualifies for one – and who is impacted on a daily basis by their anxiety, perhaps being severely restricted in how they can lead their lives.

Note that activities impacted by anxiety are sometimes difficult to determine in value by themselves, as the anxiety is often a large portion of the cost. An example could be a school day costing, in total, 2000 in the 'currency' or coinage of Energy Accounting. For a person with even mild social anxiety, the anxiety could represent 500 'coins' or more of the day's cost, depending on how many times during the day the anxiety is triggered.

● **SEE RESOURCE 7:** *Strategies That Can Cause Harm.*

## WHAT DOES USING THE ENERGY BANK LOOK LIKE?

In this section, we will present examples of visual representations of the Energy Bank and its use. If you have a different idea of how it will work better for you, do not feel that you must stick to the ways outlined here. However, when you are just beginning to learn how to use Energy Accounting, we do recommend using our templates, and then personalizing according to what suits your current needs or those of your client.

### Daily Energy Account Form

Our first and primary way to use the Energy Bank is to fill out a Daily Energy Account Form. You can draw this in a journal, type it on your phone, or use our downloadable template from Energy-Accounting.com/handouts.

Write in what the activity or event was, and on the right, its esti-mated value. Put in a value range or a set number, whichever you feel comfortable with. For the activity or event, you may choose to write it as simply as possible, or you can add more information. Optionally, you can note the time of day the activity or event took place. Some people like to note the estimated time as, for example,

2pm or 6:30am, while others prefer to note it in a more general or descriptive way, such as 'Morning' or 'Lunchbreak'.

You can get as detailed as you like, but do note that the more information included in the Daily Energy Account Form, the harder it will be to keep an overview.

*Daily Energy Account Form*

| Time | Activity/Event | Value |
|---|---|---|
| 6am | Morning routine | -40 |
| 8am | A few minutes late for school, people were looking (Situational factor) | -80 |
| 12pm | Lunchbreak, quiet area<br>Noise-cancelling headphones too! | +20–30 |
| 1pm | Favourite lesson, teacher was nice | +20 |
| 1:30pm | A friend suggested we play a computer game together after school | +40 |
| 2:30pm | Science teacher said we did not have any homework today | +30 |

Note that there can be a desire to have the daily energy account so 'well balanced' that the surplus each day is quite high, but this is often a mistake.

People generally react very poorly when they do not have enough responsibility or enough to do.

Remember that what we expect of others (and ourselves) should match the person's capacity for demands and responsibilities, and definitely not exceed it; however, it is also important that the demands are not so low that they serve to make the person feel badly about themselves, or to make them stressed.

Boredom is surprisingly stressful, feeling unchallenged can be highly stressful, and feeling expendable or as though you have nothing to contribute is highly damaging to one's self-worth, which, again, is a major stressor that can lead to depression. This means we should be looking to create a daily or weekly schedule that leaves the person feeling challenged in a positive way, useful and included.

## Cluster activities

You may have noticed the activity 'morning routine' above and wondered what that entailed. This is an example of a cluster activity and the exact contents will be different for each person. When first starting out, it may be preferable for some to be very detailed in their notes, but for others it may be overwhelming. In such a case, cluster activities may be easier to note. We would advise noting cluster activities and choosing which to look at in a more detailed way.

For many autistic people, and those with executive functioning challenges, an activity like 'morning routine' or even 'shower' may bring to mind all the details that go into it, instead of the broader concept. This can be very overwhelming to the person, and can make it difficult to cope with all the small parts that go into making daily life work. There are strategies that can make things a bit easier, but for Energy Accounting, the long-term goal is to find out which parts of the cluster activity are taking more or less energy and seek to reduce those when possible. We do this one cluster activity at a time, and try not to overwhelm the Daily Energy Account Form, or the person, with too much information.

Examples of cluster activities can be, as mentioned, 'morning routine' and 'shower', but can also be things like school or work or chores. The point of using cluster activities is to make your daily Energy Accounting easier, through reducing the amount of information. Once there is a general baseline value established for a cluster activity, only changes need to be noted.

Let's look at what the 'shower' cluster activity can look like, when expanded. This is a general example based on clinical experiences, but of course, there are likely to be differences for each person in terms of what they note as important energy withdrawals or deposits, or the order of the details.

- Taking off clothes
- Turning on water
- Checking water heat
- Getting under water, wetting hair
- Shampoo
- Body wash
- Rinse
- (Second shampooing)
- Rinse
- Conditioning hair
- Shaving
- Rinse
- Turning off water
- (Squeegee or dry walls)
- Getting out, possibly feeling cold (climate and water heat dependent)
- Drying off.

After the shower:

- Lotion (body and face)
- Hair products
- Brush and style hair
- Find and put on clean clothes.

As you can see, a lot goes into the otherwise simple task 'shower'. For someone who has their period, there are often additional steps involved, and many people may need or want to take off and/or clean jewellery as well. And if we were to include all details every day, the Daily Energy Account Form would quickly get flooded with details that would be unhelpful for anyone to spend their time writing down or estimating values for. Instead, it may be useful to only need to write the full list of a cluster activity once, and discuss which parts actually make it costly in terms of energy.

For some, this could be sensory sensitivities connected with hot or cold, or with the sound of water, for example; or it may be simply that the person cannot stop their minds from constantly going through this list and the number of steps seeming insurmountable. Once we know which aspect of an activity causes it to withdraw more energy, we can work towards finding ways to reduce the cost of the activity.

Within the cluster activity such as showering, there may be energy deposits as well as withdrawals, such as enjoying the tactile sensation of the shower and using a warm towel. Overall, the experience of having a shower may be an energy withdrawal but there could be some enjoyable aspects.

In the case of a shower, for someone with executive function challenges, it sometimes helps to have a set order in which to do each step. For others this is not sufficient, or they already have this strategy. Might it help, for example, to have the soaps and products arranged in the order they are to be used?

In the same sense, a morning routine may include these steps:

- Get up
- Go into the bathroom
- Brush teeth
- Shower
- Get dressed
- Have breakfast
- Pack bag
- Put on shoes and jacket
- Leave for school/work.

Several of these steps are, themselves, cluster activities. This goes to show how much we can stay in the 'large picture' or go into detail with Energy Accounting, depending on each person's challenges and needs.

As mentioned, once we know the baseline cost of a cluster activity, it becomes easier to note in the Daily Energy Account Form. Now, we note the cluster plus any differences from the routine.

For example:

*Daily Energy Account Form*

| Time | Activity/Event | Value |
|------|----------------|-------|
| 6am | Morning routine<br>Had favourite breakfast | -30<br>+10 |
| 8am | A few minutes late for school, people were looking (Situational factor) | -60 |
| 8am–3pm | Friend ill and not at school (-50)<br>Two hours of maths (2 x -90)<br>Break in quiet room (+10)<br>Two hours of English (-40)<br>Replacement teacher, no advance notice (-80)<br>Lunchbreak in lunch room, loud (-50)<br>Extra time in quiet room (+10)<br>Two hours of gym class (2 x -70)<br>Gym teacher made me shower at school (-100)<br>Not bullied today, relief (+20) | -600 |
| 3pm | Dad picked me up from school, change from routine (-20), but made it much easier to get home, and we listened to music in the car (+50) | +30 |
| 3.30–4pm | Quiet time in room | +30 |
| 4pm | Homework | -80 |
| 5pm | Fell asleep, good nap | +50 |
| 6pm | Dinner with family | -10 |
| 6:30pm | Alone in room, no interruptions | +80 |
| 9pm | Evening/before bed routine | -20 |

This means the daily accounting becomes more manageable over time as it becomes easier to keep an overview, and it takes less time. The Daily Energy Account Form can be used for a time period when Energy Accounting is still new to a person, and they may pick it up again later in life, during difficult periods or due to wanting to re-evaluate their daily structure. It is not intended to be used every day, non-stop for months or years. This would become a withdrawal for most people, not to mention the hours put into such an activity.

How do we know if the value estimates are flawed? The short answer is, it is a trial-and-error process. There is no 'correct' answer, it is based on personal perception. We are doing our best to find the patterns that affect well-being. If the estimates are flawed in such a way the person is running on a deficit when they believe things are properly balanced, odds are they will see stress symptoms increase over time, with the possibility that certain symptoms become very noticeable.

One of the reasons we try to use several methods together is that, often, one spots a flaw the other misses. If the Daily Energy Account looks balanced, but a simple number tracker shows imbalance over a number of weeks, the chances are there are value estimates that are off, or activities/events that have not been noted – often due to simply forgetting to note them mentally or include them in the account.

# CHAPTER 6

———————— ⟨⟨⟨⟨⟨⟩⟩⟩⟩⟩ ————

# *The Stress Threshold*

The idea of a stress threshold is quite common, and is very much tied to the idea that our energy is spent on activities throughout the day. It may be visualized in several different ways, along with the concept of withdrawals and deposits. For now, we will use a bar graph to illustrate this concept. Note that while this is useful for illustrating the stress threshold, it will not be useful for showing a realistic day in detail, as it will become confusing to look at. Therefore, when we work with this illustration, we also tend to 'zoom out' to look at a broader picture. Often, in this format, it is more useful to note cluster activities rather than details.

The stress threshold visualization is useful for discussing the consequences of stress, and for showing the various basic conditions, primary factors and situational factors that a person deals with during any given time period, and how these affect their stress levels.

The stress threshold as we use it is divided into two thresholds – the acute stress threshold and the long-term stress threshold, both of which include a warning signs line and a critical line. Think of the lines as the points in a person's capacity for stress where symptoms begin to appear – either warning signs, where the stress is still more easily managed, or critical symptoms when the stress is much more difficult to manage or treat.

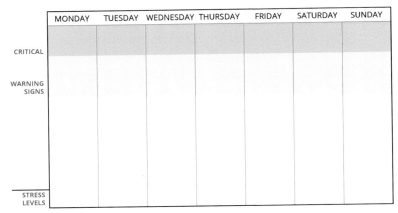

*Figure 6.1: Acute stress threshold*

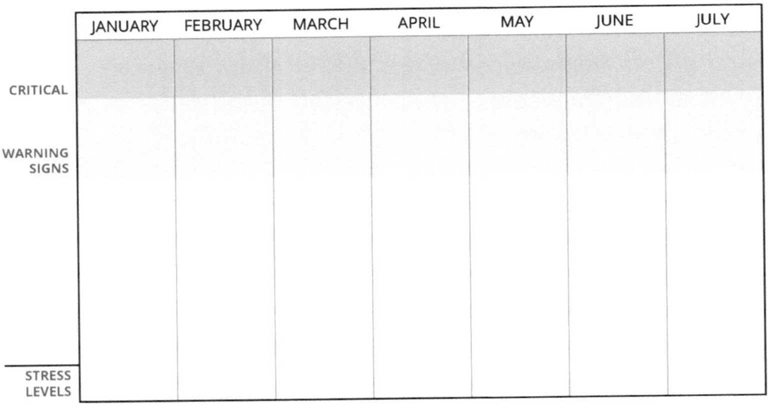

*Figure 6.2: Long-term stress threshold*

The acute stress threshold is used for discussing acute stress, focusing on single days or weeks. The long-term stress threshold is used for discussing months or years, and is often more useful for discussing how long-term factors have affected someone over a period of time and perhaps built up to cause burnout.

## ACUTE STRESS THRESHOLD
This is related to the day-to-day life in a very direct way. Crossing the warning signs line can result in, for example, minor emotional outbursts, tiredness or feeling unfocused. The reactions here may

be compared to temporarily reaching zero on the Energy Bank balance. This can happen several times a day, but the person then has access to an energy deposit such as a break in a quiet room, and is able to move forward with their day. Crossing the warning signs line may not be an issue when the person knows they are doing it and have a purpose for it. The capacity for coping with crossing this line is highly individual, and tends to increase with age and maturity.

Crossing the critical line for the acute stress threshold results in larger emotional outbursts, meltdowns, shutdowns and acute expressions of panic or anxiety, and tends to affect the person for a longer time period, often constituting a situational factor the following day. That is, crossing this line often results in needing some recovery time. However, being given this recovery time then enables the person to continue with their usual schedule for the following days or weeks, without any longer-term consequences to their mental health.

With this in mind, we would ideally plan the day and week so that neither line is crossed, knowing that surprises may happen which add stress to the day or week.

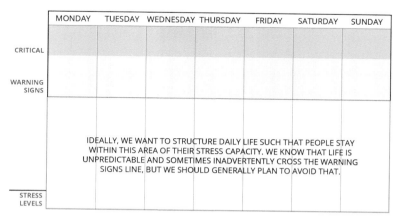

*Figure 6.3: Tolerable stress capacity*

## LONG-TERM STRESS THRESHOLD

This is a way to discuss longer time periods with regard to warning signs and critical signs of stress. In the longer term, crossing the warning signs line results in milder, but still relevant, stress symptoms. These are individual, but examples could be *minor* changes in dietary habits, hygiene habits or social behaviour. The person may, for example, still attend social activities, but less often, or they may be quieter than they used to be. At home with family, they may be slightly more irritable. They may sleep a bit more than they used to, or have a harder time getting out of bed in the morning. These are definite signs that something has changed for that person, but they do not yet reach the level of clinical significance. We would argue that when such signs are noticed, this is a great time to make changes to reduce stress in that person's life, as changes at this point see much quicker results. The person is far more likely to be 'back to their former selves' within weeks or months when we intervene at this point than if we wait.

Often, what happens is that these warning signs are not recognized as warning signs, and the person continues to build up stress until they cross the long-term critical stress threshold. At this point, long-term consequences affect physical health and psychological well-being. The critical threshold is the point at which serious and concerning symptoms show themselves. By the time a person crosses the long-term stress threshold, outbursts, meltdowns, shutdowns and other acute stress symptoms are likely to have become far more common. Children may develop school refusal, and adults often show concerning psychological and physiological symptoms. At this point of stress, we see psychiatric and medical diagnoses develop or worsen. For example, there can be a development or worsening of anxiety, depression, sleep disorders, frequent physiological symptoms such as stomach aches, severe headaches, muscle tension, dizziness or changes in vision. One of the primary concerns of Energy Accounting is to never reach this critical point if it is possible to avoid it. For that reason, we keep this threshold in mind even though it is not the one we focus on in the active use of this method.

When considering these stress thresholds, it is important to remember that people's capacity to cope with stressors changes greatly depending on circumstances, maturity and resilience. Many factors affect this change in capacity, some of which may be predicted, others not. Estimating exactly where a person's stress thresholds lie is difficult, and most often a trial-and-error process. With that noted, the value of activities can be shown on the graph in this way.

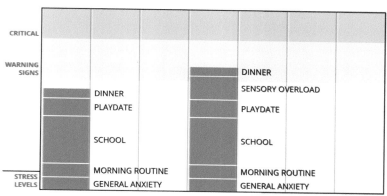

*Figure 6.4: Example stress threshold with basic
conditions and situational factors*

As mentioned, it is often more useful to work with cluster activities within the graph illustration. Furthermore, because it is difficult to work in any significant degree of detail, it tends to work better as a way to explain how certain factors can push you over the threshold, rather than as a tool to track whether a day is balanced or not.

## RESIDUAL OVERLOAD

Some people feel that the deficit from one day 'transfers' to the next. They may have their own ways of marking this, and again we advise to use whichever way makes sense to the person. We have seen most success clinically with marking this on the graph by adding a situational factor on the following day, often called 'residual deficit', 'residual overload' or 'tiredness'.

As the graph shows, in this particular case, sensory overload on Tuesday caused the 'warning signs' line to be crossed, creating a residual overload the following day which amplified the person's anxiety greatly. This unfortunately caused somewhat of a ripple effect for the following days, and we can see that their schedule should have been adjusted probably on Wednesday to avoid further overload. On Friday, the person stayed home from school to reduce stress, and no more playdates were scheduled for that week. It was also agreed that any homework would only be reviewed on Sunday. This enabled them to recover for the following Monday.

| | MONDAY | TUESDAY | WEDNESDAY | THURSDAY | FRIDAY | SATURDAY | SUNDAY |
|---|---|---|---|---|---|---|---|
| CRITICAL | | | | | | | |
| | | | DINNER | | | | |
| WARNING SIGNS | | DINNER | SENSORY OVERLOAD | DINNER | | | |
| | HOMEWORK | SENSORY OVERLOAD | PLAYDATE | | | | |
| | DINNER | | | SCHOOL | DINNER | | DINNER |
| | PLAYDATE | PLAYDATE | SCHOOL | | MORNING ROUTINE | DINNER | HOMEWORK |
| | SCHOOL | SCHOOL | MORNING ROUTINE | MORNING ROUTINE | ANXIETY (Residual overload) | MORNING ROUTINE | MORNING ROUTINE |
| | MORNING ROUTINE | MORNING ROUTINE | ANXIETY (Residual overload) | ANXIETY (Residual overload) | | ANXIETY (Residual overload) | ANXIETY |
| | ANXIETY | ANXIETY | | | | | |

*Figure 6.5: Example of residual overload*

Crossing the warning signs line on a daily basis causes the residual overload to grow, or other activities to increase in value, such that cumulative stress builds. In many cases, this happens so gradually that we do not notice until a critical line is crossed, either the acute or the long-term. However, there is the further complication that some people, especially autistic people, may have delayed processing, such that symptoms of having crossed a stress threshold line occur at a delayed time. In most cases, the delay will be minutes or hours, but we have seen cases where symptoms of stress occur days, weeks or even months after the events or changes which truly caused stress to accumulate. This makes intervening much more difficult, and, indeed, makes it much harder to identify the source of the stress. However, once the person shows symptoms, they are more likely to either be able to communicate what is stressing them, or they react situationally to the factor.

## THE EFFECTS OF LONG-TERM STRESS OR BURNOUT

In a situation where the deficit continues and there is no room for recharging and stabilizing the situation, stress builds and the impact on the person's brain and nervous system – over time – causes sensitization to stressors, agitating or triggering mental health or physical health problems. This happens over the course of months or even years, before the person is affected to such a degree that they may no longer be able to function on a daily basis and is forced to leave school or work. Visually, we can leave the thresholds as they are and add factors to the graph, or we may illustrate the lower capacity for stressors by lowering the thresholds.

These two graphs illustrate how these two options would look, without taking into account the changes that would need to occur in the person's life. In both instances, we see that major changes need to happen in order for recovery to take place.

Furthermore, in cases of burnout, we also see that the distance between the acute warning signs and critical lines shrinks. In plain English, the person is more prone to feeling very acutely stressed, very quickly.

People may differ greatly on which illustration they prefer, and as with everything else, we encourage the person to focus on whichever makes most sense to them.

| | MONDAY | TUESDAY | WEDNESDAY | THURSDAY | FRIDAY | SATURDAY | SUNDAY |
|---|---|---|---|---|---|---|---|
| | | DINNER | | | | | |
| CRITICAL | | | | | | | |
| | | SENSORY OVERLOAD | | | | | |
| WARNING SIGNS | DINNER | | | | | | |
| | PLAYDATE | PLAYDATE | | | | | |
| | SCHOOL | SCHOOL | | | | | |
| | MORNING ROUTINE | MORNING ROUTINE | | | | | |
| | ANXIETY | ANXIETY | | | | | |
| | BURNOUT | BURNOUT | | | | | |

| | MONDAY | TUESDAY | WEDNESDAY | THURSDAY | FRIDAY | SATURDAY | SUNDAY |
|---|---|---|---|---|---|---|---|
| CRITICAL | | DINNER | | | | | |
| | | SENSORY OVERLOAD | | | | | |
| | DINNER | | | | | | |
| | PLAYDATE | PLAYDATE | | | | | |
| WARNING SIGNS | | | | | | | |
| | SCHOOL | SCHOOL | | | | | |
| | MORNING ROUTINE | MORNING ROUTINE | | | | | |
| | ANXIETY | ANXIETY | | | | | |

*Figure 6.6: Example of long-term stress or burnout*

However, it is essential to understand that the stress threshold lines *can* move, and especially that the distance between the acute warning signs and critical lines can differ over time. There may be maturity factors, hormonal factors and much else such as physical health, and while we *could* note these as primary or situational factors on the graph, when they are more long-term it can make more sense to illustrate them by having a different distance between the warning signs and critical lines.

When our nervous systems are functioning effectively there is room between the acute warning signs and critical lines – meaning we have a higher capacity for stressors in daily life. More importantly, we are more resilient to stress, meaning that even hitting the acute critical line will not have quite so severe consequences in terms of emotional outbursts, meltdowns, shutdowns, anxiety attacks, withdrawal or other reactions. Instead, while we still do react, we are more able to adapt and continue to cope.

For people with chronic anxiety or severe depressions or autistic people who have been pressured from a very young age to live up to non-autistic expectations, it is entirely possible that their Energy Accounting process begins at a time when their acute critical line is very close to the warning signs line. Moreover, they may still be pushing themselves to the edge of their capacity each day. The result can be that any improvement they have experienced so far is due to changes in maturity, but often what happens is that there is no improvement, and they lose hope. The way out of this pattern is to recognize that even with correct treatment and strategies such as Energy Accounting, it takes time for the person's nervous system to recover, and in order to do so, their stress capacity or acute stress threshold must be continuously respected. As a metaphor, we might say that allowing some distance from the acute warning signs threshold gives the brain and nervous system room to spend the extra energy healing itself. This is why Energy Accounting focuses on the acute stress threshold to the degree that it does. In effect, we want to avoid reaching that threshold whenever possible. However, we do recognize that, at times, it will be impossible to avoid severe stressors, and the stress responses associated with those can affect Energy Accounting for some days or even weeks following.

The point to be made is that it is okay to not be able to return to 'normal' just after a stressor that is significant to that person. We want to encourage acceptance that recovering after subjectively severe or strong stressors is something that takes time. People can experience a degree of shame that they are not able to 'just move on', and in such cases, it is important that the person is able to forgive themselves for not being able to do that, and for not having the resilience they expect of themselves. Perhaps it can help to know that it is normal to need time to recover, even if the stressor was acute in nature.

## DAILY FLUCTUATIONS

Additionally, when looking only at one day at a time, we see clinically that people's capacity for stressors can be spread out very differently across a day. This is often connected to how much perceived energy they have.

Often, this capacity is greatest around the earlier hours of the day and slowly declines over the afternoon and evening, as though the energy is 'leaking' through the day. For some people, however, mornings may be the time of day where they need to build up this capacity, and if changes happen in their morning routine, they are 'stuck' at a high stress level, close to the acute threshold, for the remainder of the day.

For exploring this, we recommend using the tools discussed in Chapter 4, Monitoring Well-Being. Specifically, it can be useful to fill out the chart tracking daily fluctuations using the preferred system.

For example, using the battery system or a simple number system, we might see a pattern over a few weeks. Often, the pattern will be different during weekdays and weekends, as there are often more activities planned during weekdays which cost energy. However, this is not always the case.

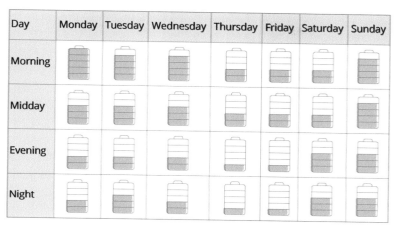

*Figure 6.7: Battery tracking*

## INDIVIDUAL DIFFERENCES

Each person's capacity to cope with stressors is different and will change throughout their life. There will be increases and decreases in capacity, changes in when stress symptoms appear, to what degree, and what form they take.

Noticing a change in capacity usually occurs through the appearance of stress symptoms when they are not expected, or the lack thereof when they *are* expected. For this reason, a part of the exploration stage focuses on identifying individual stress symptoms (see Chapter 2 for the table of stress symptoms).

It is important to assess symptoms in accordance with the person's usual behaviour, taking into account symptoms of any relevant diagnoses and the side effects of any medication. For an autistic person, social isolation as a symptom of stress should take into account their usual social life, social circle and the level of social interaction they are usually comfortable with during periods where they are not stressed. That is, remember that being alone does not necessarily equate to feeling lonely, and that having a limited social circle may not equate to being isolated or isolating oneself.

If we consider a person's capacity for coping with stressors to be spread out over the day, we may then see that stress symptoms can appear at times where the acute warning signs threshold is crossed only momentarily. That is, a stressful situation may increase their heart rate, blood pressure, and so on, but once they are away from the situation and their adrenaline levels go down, they may still have energy to go about (most of) the rest of the day. There may be some rumination on the event later which adds an energy cost, but for the most part, they are okay. In effect, the acute warning signs threshold has been crossed, but recovery can take place during that same day – that is, if we zoomed in on this particular day rather than the week, we would see in their mental 'graph' the stress level fluctuations during the day and this would show as a high peak, after which the stress level slowly decreases. Zooming out to the week-view we would see that the acute stress threshold was crossed minimally, but we would not see the time of day it happened, nor the subsequent recovery.

Events like these may be more rare or frequent, depending on many factors, but it is unavoidable that they will occur once in a while. Using Energy Accounting will not prevent them from happening. However, what we can do is try to budget the energy such that an event like this is more easily recovered from. This can be strengthened by psychoeducation, increased self-awareness and self-understanding, and having a number of strategies available that the person can use in such situations.

A person's ability to recover is dependent on many factors, including age/maturity, cognitive functions, and the frequency with which their stress thresholds are crossed. Note here that cognitive function declines with factors like tiredness or intoxication. A person who does not get sufficient sleep or quality sleep will have this as a factor in their day, which means they are closer to the acute warning signs threshold, but it also impacts their ability to think of solutions to a problem and their ability to regulate their emotions, which means their access to the strategies they need to recover is reduced. So people who have factors in their lives that impact them in this way are more likely to stay at a high level of stress once either of the acute thresholds have been crossed. In the example of poor or too little sleep, it may be a simple situational factor – having slept poorly on that particular night – or it can be a primary or basic factor in that person's life – being a light sleeper, having an infant/toddler who keeps them awake or interrupts their sleep a lot, or perhaps having a chronic sleep disorder, such as sleep apnoea.

As we can see, there can be individual differences in how well a person recovers from stressors which are not dependent on simply balancing the numbers. Some people need to have their days planned in a way that makes it less likely that their thresholds are crossed than others, not only due to having additional stress factors in their lives – and thus, lower capacity for coping with situational stressors – but also due to factors which are difficult to put into an accounting format.

As noted earlier, some people are also more resilient than others. The term resilience carries with it its own debate, and, as we have stated, we do not necessarily believe that people who can handle a lot of situational factors are more resilient than those who cannot – the second group likely has more basic and primary factors which deplete their stress capacity. When we talk about resilience in this book, we are referring to how well and for how long a person can cope with pushing themselves to their stress capacity limit. Some people seem to have further between their warning signs and critical thresholds than others, and this is likely to do with how healthy or balanced their nervous system is – and not to neglect mentioning it, their age, because as explained in the chapter on stress, adult organisms have better capacity to adapt to stress than young ones do.

## STABILIZING THE STRESS CAPACITY

Stress capacity can be loosely conceptualized as the capacity left over at any given time, after basic and primary factors are taken into account. That is, how far is there from these factors to the acute and critical thresholds?

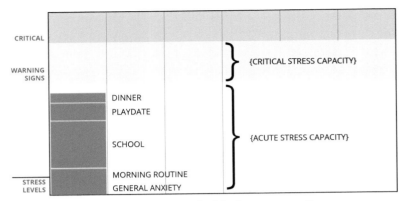

*Figure 6.8: Acute and critical stress capacity*

One of the central parts of Energy Accounting is to stabilize the acute stress capacity as much as possible. This does not mean that we never challenge ourselves or want to improve, instead it means that our approach to improving involves first building a good foundation from which we can challenge ourselves. For the moment, consider blood sugar: if you have a healthy diet, your blood sugar will still have fluctuations throughout the day but these will be relatively small and take place over a longer period of time. In comparison, if you consume a lot of sweet foods which have very little fibre, your blood sugar will tend to have more peaks and lows, or perhaps sharper peaks, fluctuating relatively quickly. This is one way to conceptualize how one's stress capacity changes throughout the day or week.

In both cases, there will be fluctuations. There is a degree of instability which cannot be avoided and this is okay. Our aim is to stabilize as much as possible, within reason and taking into account the individual's needs, abilities and goals. People are often not able or willing to do everything that might help to stabilize their stress capacity and they may have many different reasons for this. Our approach is to educate non-judgementally on which possibilities there are, and support any changes people wish to make.

Generally speaking, there are five aspects of life to focus on when attempting to stabilize the stress capacity, some of which must be implemented for longer periods of time before we can expect to see any real changes:

- Diet
- Exercise
- Sleep
- Positive experiences and good deeds
- Community/social life.

Each of these influences the production or conversion of neurotransmitters we need to feel better, at one or another step of the process, and they are essential to allowing our body, nervous system and brain to function optimally.

Our nervous system is affected by our physical health, including what we eat, how much we move, how we sleep, and so on. Everything we do and experience causes a change in the neurotransmitters and hormones which affect so greatly how we feel.

There is a narrative in society that getting healthy – eating healthy food, exercising, sleep, and so on – is simple and that people should just stop being lazy and do it. This is, of course, not the truth. There are foods that are unhealthy but which trick our brains into wanting more. Many people are made to be stationary either at work or school for many hours per day, not using their bodies but instead becoming tired from constantly needing to process information, learn and solve problems. Having the energy to exercise or cook healthy meals can be a very serious challenge – and this is without addressing any financial barriers there may be. However, we are not trying to change everything all at once. When examining ways to stabilize your stress capacity, or that of the person you are helping, start small.

Generally speaking, we can only change one habit at a time, and it is much easier to make a new habit than to remove an old one. Furthermore, it is easier to make a new habit by 'piggybacking' on another. For example, if you were someone who did not floss your teeth and you wanted to start flossing, it is much easier to piggyback the flossing habit on your tooth-brushing habit, rather than flossing at a different time of day, or flossing before brushing your teeth. This is not to say that creating the new habit will be easy, but piggybacking habits onto others is still *easier* for most people than creating a new, standalone habit.

# CHAPTER 7

*Colour-Coding System*

As explained earlier in the book, it emerged during the development of Energy Accounting that it may be beneficial to divide energy into several, interconnected types or categories of energy, which all need to balance out. Some are acute or short-term energies, others much more subtle, long-term ones. These contribute to stabilizing the stress capacity or act as a 'buffer' against stress, anxiety and depression.

To indicate these different types or categories of energy, it can be useful to colour code them as they correspond to cost and deposits, using the colours that make sense for each individual.

Colour coding is especially useful when planning a schedule, or indeed, re-examining an existing one.

Examples of categories that may be used to colour code for types of energy:

- Restoring – special interest time, solitude, relaxation, activities that are a highly valued deposit for the person.
- Social – when the activity is inherently social, but not to such an extent that it is in the draining category. Often these are activities like playdates, a small and short family gathering, a one-to-one conversation with a friend or colleague.
- Physical – exercise/movement, food/nutrition, sleep. Anything to do with physical health.
- Mental – these activities often take place in solitude, but do

not need to. Reading, writing assignments but also activities like Sudoku puzzles, chess or other games that require focused problem solving.

- Draining – any type of activity that drains energy to a large extent. These are often large social events, or activities that take up most of their day. Note that every activity in this category is not necessarily draining to the same degree! This colour is often a guide to when days off or restoring activities are needed. Often these are cluster activities such as school, and while adults may not always put work in this category, often events such as training courses or conferences do fit well here.

- Sensory – for those with sensory processing differences, it can make sense to have a separate category for sensory experiences, both positive and negative. Some prefer to have two colours for this category or split them into two categories, but this is highly individual, as is the use of the category.

- Other – if no other category really fits, put it here, or create your own category if needed.

- Take care – this category is used to mark times of year that the stress capacity is decreased. In some ways, learning to use this category requires good self-understanding and reflection. In others, it is relatively simple. For example, seasonal allergies could be marked during the months where they are an issue. If a person is prone to seasonal depressions or something similar, that should go in this category, too.

When exploring colour coding, use categories as they make sense for you or the person you work with. If you don't want to use the suggested categories, it can be well worth inventing your own as well! The important part is for it to make sense for the individual.

It is important to note that no colour should be seen as inherently negative or positive; rather, the colours are meant only to portray information. We have seen cases where people interpret the 'draining' category as meaning 'anything negative', but it should not be so. Draining activities are not necessarily ones that make you feel emotionally bad, or that put you in a bad mood. They are simply activities that 'cost more'. Examples, depending on one's personality and current stress situation, could be: going to the cinema, shopping for groceries, going to a large event, hosting or attending a birthday party, travel involving large train stations or airports.

Note that these activities almost always include interaction with large numbers of people. Very often, draining activities are ones that either require great focus or involve lots of sensory input, and often they do this in combination with a social activity. For this reason, attending school or work is often a draining activity, even if it involves restoring aspects, such as a favourite class or a special interest.

It is especially helpful in lengthy cluster activities such as school or work to examine the 'micro' picture. What is draining and restoring about the day? To examine this, we would start exploring the cluster activity in more detail, assigning values and potentially categories/colours as it makes sense to the person.

## RESTORING

In this book, restoring activities will be marked with GREEN in examples.

Restoring activities have a short- and long-term function, as many categories do. Mainly, they contribute to mental well-being by creating feelings of joy, calm, safety and fulfilment. Used well, they contribute to achieving as stable a stress capacity as possible – note that achieving complete stability is not considered an end goal, as lives generally go through changes on a regular basis and these will influence the stress capacity as well.

In the short term, restoring activities are often used well for acute balancing of other activities. For example, when draining activities or social activities have brought someone close to their threshold, having access to a special interest can quickly bring the stress levels back down.

In the long term, following that logic, restoring activities can be used to make sure there is a steady inflow into the accounts through activities that contribute directly to well-being. They provide a positive aspect to focus on even during times filled with stress or pressure, as thinking about a restoring activity you have completed or have scheduled for later will for many people bring some momentary joy or relaxation. When implementing Energy Accounting with an adult, having a planned longer time period (several hours, a half day, a day) for restoring activities can be the promise of restoration that a person needs to get through a few tough days or even weeks. In this way, some restoring activities can have 'tails', in the sense that looking forward to something restoring, or having just experienced a great restoring activity, can provide an energy boost for the days before or after an activity. This mostly applies to higher value restoring activities, and those which have a longer timeframe.

However, restoring activities can be short in duration, too, and still have great effect. For many, taking five to ten minutes to do something energy infusing for themselves can make a big difference to their day. This could be making a cup of their favourite tea, or finding something pretty in nature to take a picture of; it can even be writing a gratitude journal. For others, and especially younger people, a restoring activity can also involve finding a short video of something relating to an interest.

## SOCIAL
In this book, social activities will be marked with RED in examples.

This type of activity is a double-edged sword for autistic people, introverts and others who find socializing difficult. In the short and long term, these activities often drain energy in fairly large quantities, depending on the sensory environment they take place in and the familiarity and attitudes of the participants. However, even the calmest social activity, adjusted to protect the autistic person as much as possible, usually drains energy in the short term. Note that the person or people involved makes a difference as well. Being social for the same amount of time with two different people tends to result in two different costs. Additionally, different contexts or activities influence the cost as well. Some people drain your energy while others infuse you with energy.

In the long term, however, social activity protects against loneliness. For this reason, social activities should be seen as necessary for good mental health. It is important to note that the amount and the type of social activity should be adjusted to the individual's social capacity and abilities. One person may need to speak in person or on the phone with someone for 30 minutes once a day or every other day, another may need only to have only five minutes of online chatting per week, and yet another may be fine with a support person or animal being in the room but with no more interaction than that. People's capacity for social interaction is very individual, and may also change throughout their lifespan and as a friendship or relationship matures. The development or treatment of, for example, social anxiety will also make a difference in social confidence and general perceived energy depletion or infusion.

When working with autistic people, people with social anxiety, introverts or others for whom social interaction is an energy costly activity, we must be very sure to use social activities to benefit the mental health of the individual, not to push them as far as is possible, as this will turn social interaction into something that induces anxiety or stress and avoidance of social experiences to a larger extent than is necessary.

Note also that, sometimes, people want to be social more than they actually have the energy for. A child may want more playdates or longer playdates, but the parent will know from experience that allowing this will result in a meltdown at home. It is also possible for many to be social for longer than what is strictly needed, but again, do be mindful of keeping the activity limited to avoid pushing beyond the stress capacity, either short or long term. Prior to a social gathering, it may be helpful to determine the current social capacity and energy levels and set a time limit for social participation based on that information. If there are difficulties with the perception of time and stress levels, a smartphone or smartwatch can be set to indicate when it is time to start to leave.

Used well, regular social activities will serve to increase happiness by protecting against loneliness and giving access to positive social experiences. The difficulty is finding the right balance and the right people.

Social activities act as a buffer against stress by providing oxytocin. This only happens if the person is comfortable and feels safe. Oxytocin is produced when we experience touch, eye contact and a sense of togetherness, connectedness and community. Oxytocin can also be produced by interacting with animals, so if the only time a person feels safe and comfortable being social is with their pet, then this is where they will get oxytocin – at least for the time being. It is possible to learn to feel more comfortable and safe in social interactions with people, but it will be a slow process, and someone who does not like being social with people does not tend to become a social butterfly.

For autistic people, communities that are related to their interests tend to be easier to connect with, as the trouble of finding things to talk about is removed, there may be less small talk, and people do not react negatively as often if they continue to talk about the shared interest at length. Often, what happens in these communities is that the person has the opportunity to discover others who are genuinely interested in and listen to their experiences and perspectives, and relate to and validate their thoughts and feelings.

Always remember to focus on interactions where there are feelings of safety and being comfortable. Being able to relax allows a person to have that positive social experience and discover what it feels like to have a sense of community and connectedness with others.

## High social motivation as a risk factor

It used to be the general perception that autistic people were uninterested in social interaction, but in fact, some autistic people have a very high motivation and desire to be social. However, this does not mean that being social is easy for them – in fact, they still have all the social difficulties and challenges that come with autism.

Some use masking or mimicking as a social strategy, which means they spend a lot of effort hiding or suppressing autistic behaviours intellectually rather than intuitively creating a social persona and script. This social 'mask' becomes a considerable drain on the Energy Bank account and can lead to meltdowns or even contribute to burnout and depression. Aside from this, there is also a risk of the person feeling disappointed in themselves when they fail to uphold the mask or mimicking strategy.

## PHYSICAL

In this book, physical activities will be marked with BLUE in examples.

Many autistic people find themselves at one extreme or the other when it comes to physical activity. Some love sports so much they make a career of it or they at least engage in sporting or intense physical activities several times a week, and others dislike or are unable to engage in typical physical activities. For those who love it, this can be an extra energy-restoring category, and for those who consider physical activity as aversive, it will be very difficult indeed to consider physical activity as a source of energy. One of the reasons people sometimes avoid physical activity such as sports is the derogatory comments from peers during childhood regarding physical coordination, abilities such as running, catching a ball and physical endurance. This can lead the person to have a low sense of confidence when it comes to these types of activities and there can be an increased vulnerability to being ridiculed.

However, this category is not just about sports. It is all activities related to physical health, including movement, as well as nutrition, personal hygiene and sleep. All of these need to be balanced in daily life in order to protect a person's physical and mental health. We are not advocating for any extreme physical health programme. This category should, in many ways, be treated the same as the social category. Activities in this category may very well be costly in the short term, but still be very beneficial in the long term, especially for achieving better stability in the stress capacity, or as a 'buffer' against stress. If the option is practically and financially available, it may be worthwhile for individuals to seek the advice of a personal trainer to design a physical activity programme based on their body type, personality and previous physical activity experience. The activities do not need to take place at a gym.

In the same manner, it may be necessary to find strategies for how personal hygiene and nutrition are best maintained personally, without feeling as if it is too much of a withdrawal in the moment. This will allow for longer-term benefits, but with fewer acute 'withdrawal fees'.

Importantly, keep in mind that goals for any changes should be realistic for the individual. There is no reason to think everyone will be able to eat an optimal diet or exercise for an hour each day. The idea is to make gradual changes the person feels ready and excited for, which can contribute to a balance in neurotransmitters and overall physical health.

For those who are, due to various reasons, unable to feel good about leaving their homes or even their rooms, physical movement is difficult to come by. In such cases, we recommend introducing any version of movement the person can cope with. This may be virtual reality computer games or other games that involve movement, or it can be installing an exercise bike at home. Often, the first way to practise leaving the home for exercise that becomes viable is to walk outside with a pet. We recognize that these examples assume able-bodiedness, and anyone who is not able-bodied will need alternatives depending on their specific circumstances.

## MENTAL

In this book, mental activities will be marked with TEAL in examples.

Mental activities are, like physical ones, either loved or abhorred. Whereas some people cherish brain puzzles, studying, reading and so on, others find it dull or difficult. However, for most people, their lives include some amount of mental activities. There is usually either homework to do, projects to complete, budgeting or some other form of activity which requires one's full mental attention and challenges one's cognitive abilities to some degree. These activities are often physically stationary, which means they do not contribute to physical health, as generally understood. However, they often contribute to well-being, although often indirectly. For example, budgeting contributes to financial stability, which can lessen anxiety. Homework contributes to learning and advancing in education, which can heighten a sense of achievement and self-esteem.

Sometimes, activities like homework prompt thoughts of being incompetent or less-than, in which case the activities have a significantly larger cost, perhaps becoming draining ones. In this situation, we recommend trying to find mental activities that can do the reverse – build up confidence and excitement for learning – even if this is in another field altogether. Importantly, mental activities should not be considered draining simply for being unwanted activities – they may be difficult or boring, but the degree of the energy cost will vary depending on the activity. If someone finds maths easy but reading difficult, the deposit or cost will differ but they both remain in this category. If that same person becomes anxious from having to complete a particular assignment, it may be wise to have restoring activities following completion.

The issue with mental activities is that, for those who do not like them, the pay-off often seems very distant, if it is even recognized. For that reason, these activities may be very costly in the short term. The goal in such a case is to manage the cost or take advantage of the deposits in such a way that the person can overcome their daily and weekly life, while building a sense of achievement.

Mental activities can also include acquiring information on a special interest. The acquisition, retention and ability to recall and enjoy the information can be a very effective source of energy. The autistic mind often needs and seeks information as an enjoyable intellectual exercise, but also as a source of self-identity and connection to those who share the same interests.

Another mental activity is finding the solution to a puzzle such as a crossword, code word or word search, which can provide a sense of accomplishment and demonstration of intellectual ability.

Another source of mental energy, emotional stability and mental clarity is meditation. There are many methods of meditation and the benefits can be considerable in terms of energy restoration but also learning to guide and manage one's own attention, including lapses in attention, which is a useful skill for the entire lifespan.

Mental activities also include art, crafts and music. These can be restoring activities as well, but for those who are interested in the history or analysis of these topics, or perhaps creating their own art, the mental immersion in the activity could place it within this category as well. Aside from having the potential to be a positive mental activity, engaging with and creating various types of art can also be a means of exploring and expressing emotions, a method of achieving greater self-understanding and appreciation, a way to be recognized for your talent and creativity, a source of self-worth and possibly income, and a way to find a community with like-minded individuals. The potential benefits of engaging with art are vast and should not be overlooked.

## DRAINING

In this book, draining activities will be marked with PINK in examples.

This category is perhaps the most difficult, as it can contain quite varying activities, some of which may also belong to other categories such as socializing, and also may not contain activities one might first assume it should. Any examples of draining activities given in this book should be considered as mere examples, as the activities in this category can vary widely from person to person. Every person will have their unique profile of energy-draining and restoring experiences, and the value of each will vary slightly from day to day.

Generally speaking, draining activities are the activities that result in acute anxiety, stress or meltdowns within a week or so unless counter-acted with restoring activities, but sometimes within as short a time span as seconds. The shorter the timespan, the easier they are to recognize. Often, with the draining activities that result in immediate stress reactions, we find that the usual coping mechanisms no longer work to alleviate the stress. In these cases, it seems to take a while before the adrenaline wears off enough for strategies to be effective again.

Draining activities overall tend to result in high levels of stress, and often an obvious or prolonged stress response. However, we urge readers to remember that some autistic people will express stress and distress in different ways or have difficulties expressing it at all.

Another type of draining activity can be large cluster activities. These are activities that take up a large amount of the person's stress capacity for the day.

Draining activities are also quite often unforeseen events, which makes things rather difficult to plan around. However, as the book will hopefully demonstrate, there is a purpose to tracking them anyway. As for the ones that can be foreseen, they may be experiences like exams, large social events such as school/work parties or family holidays, or travelling to and arriving at an entirely new location. Being able to foresee that such events will drain large amounts of energy means we are also able to plan for restoring activities in order to counter the expenditure. These can be before a known event, to increase the acute stress capacity, or afterwards, to restore the energy that has been spent. Be aware that, as with other categories, draining activities do not all cost the same, and that time spent on draining versus restoring activities often is not one to one when the purpose is to recover from draining activities.

Recovery often takes longer, depending on how effective the restoring activities are and how draining the activity or event was.

| | MONDAY | TUESDAY | WEDNESDAY | THURSDAY | FRIDAY | SATURDAY | SUNDAY |
|---|---|---|---|---|---|---|---|
| CRITICAL | | | DINNER | | | | |
| WARNING SIGNS | | DINNER | SENSORY OVERLOAD | DINNER | | | |
| | DINNER | SENSORY OVERLOAD | PLAYDATE | PLAYDATE | | | |
| | PLAYDATE | PLAYDATE | SCHOOL | SCHOOL | | | |
| | SCHOOL | SCHOOL | MORNING ROUTINE | MORNING ROUTINE | | | |
| | MORNING ROUTINE | MORNING ROUTINE | ANXIETY (Residual overload) | ANXIETY (Residual overload) | | | |
| | ANXIETY | ANXIETY | | | | | |

A SENSORY OVERLOAD CAN BE SEVERE ENOUGH THAT ITS EFFECTS ECHO FOR SEVERAL DAYS AFTER THE EVENT, INFLUENCING THE COMING DAYS WITH A LOWERED THRESHOLD/CAPACITY TO HANDLE OTHERWISE RELATIVELY PEACEFUL EVENTS.

*Figure 7.1: Cluster and sensory activity example*

It is important to note that reaching a meltdown or shutdown can be a drain on the person's energy economy by itself. In a sense, the meltdown or shutdown can have a residual cost over several days, almost like an interest or a bill to be paid. This skews the

Energy Accounting for the coming days, meaning that changes have to be made.

## SENSORY

In this book, sensory activities will be marked with ORANGE in examples.

This category tends to be beneficial to those who are more influenced, positively and negatively, by sensory experiences than most. The use of the category is highly individual, and some even prefer to have two categories rather than one – one for positive sensory experiences, and one for negative, each with their own colour coding. While some people prefer to have sensory experiences included in the Restoring and Draining categories, this does not make sense for others.

Another way this category can be useful is during exploration of one's Energy Accounting. If a diary or journal is kept of daily energy deposits and withdrawals during a week or two, details about the days may be noted. We find that many people do not fully realize the extent to which sensory experiences impact their stress and anxiety levels, and noting events as they happen can sometimes play a big role in self-discovery in this regard, as well as in others.

In clinical cases where parents are the primary source of information, a therapist or other professional may aid the discovery process by asking for details regarding the person's responses to sensory experiences. Often, we find details that are unexpected.

## OTHER

In this book, non-categorized activities will be marked with DARK GREEN in examples.

Regardless of one's best intentions to categorize and label everything, there will always be something that falls outside these labels and categories; for example, something that is unique or personal for the individual. Examples of these may be scarce, as an argument can often be made of them belonging to one or another category. The purpose of this category is mainly to have a colour available that distinguishes non-categorized activities from plain information, which is often kept in plain black text. An activity can be categorized as 'other' while one is uncertain of how to categorize it.

## TAKE CARE

In this book, 'take care' periods will be marked with PURPLE in examples.

This category may not apply to everyone, but many people do have periods where they can predict that their stress capacity will be lower, for example during and recovering from an illness. During these times, one can adjust by planning more time for restoring activities to balance things, declining to do other activities or postponing them if possible, in order to lower the amount of energy spent in the first place.

These periods may differ greatly from person to person, but some common examples may be winter months, pollen seasons, exam periods, pre-menstrual or menstrual periods, the month or months surrounding a move or change of work or school environment, or the anniversary of a traumatic experience or grief for a family member or pet who died. Less predictable examples may be the days following a meltdown, or a longer timeframe following a break-up or the death of someone close. Note that the grieving process can be delayed for autistic individuals or others with tendencies towards delayed processing. As such, you may see that the stress capacity remains stable for a few weeks or even months, after which a collapse occurs.

# EXAMPLES

We include here a few examples of how colour coding can be used in Energy Accounting, both for exploration – detective work, in a sense – and for planning.

The examples provided here may be very different from what is realistic for you or for each person you work with, and so the example values should not be taken as a guide for what is true or optimal but rather as merely ideas for how it can look.

Going back to the Daily Energy Account Form, we can now colour in each activity, showing what the day actually looks like.

*Daily Energy Account Form*

| Time | Activity/Event | Value |
|------|----------------|-------|
| 6am | Morning routine<br>Had favourite breakfast | -30<br>+10 |
| 8am | A few minutes late for school, people were looking (Situational factor) | -60 |
| 8am–3pm | Friend ill and not at school (-50)<br>Two hours of maths (2 x -90)<br>Recess in quiet room (+10)<br>Two hours of English (-40)<br>Replacement teacher, no advance notice (-80)<br>Lunchbreak in lunch room, loud (-50)<br>Extra time in quiet room (+10)<br>Two hours of gym class (2 x -70)<br>Gym teacher made me shower at school (-100)<br>Not bullied today, relief (+20) | -600 |
| 3pm | Dad picked me up from school, change from routine (-20), but made it much easier to get home, and we listened to music in the car (+50) | +30 |
| 3:30–4pm | Quiet time in room | +30 |
| 4pm | Homework | -80 |
| 5pm | Fell asleep, good nap | +50 |
| 6pm | Dinner with family | -10 |
| 6:30pm | Alone in room, no interruptions | +80 |
| 9pm | Evening/before bed routine | -20 |

We see that the day is quite diverse in categories, but we also see that several of the restoring activities are changes from the norm. Furthermore, we see that while there are plenty of blue, physical health-related activities, none of them require movement or even sunlight. This sort of information can be easier to spot when using colour coding, provided the many colours are not confusing to the eye – which of course they can be to some people.

If we examine the simplified graph showing activities from Chapter 6, The Stress Threshold, we see now that the example activities are overwhelmingly draining. Furthermore, there are no restoring activities built in. There are mental activities, as they would be a part of school, and we might assume there are brief restoring activities now and again. However, this very picture demonstrates why it is difficult to show restoring activities in this type of visual representation – if we put the restoring activities in, the person would appear to have increased stress levels from them, not decreased. For this reason, this graph visualization is rarely used to track what an actual day may look like. Instead, it may be used to discuss where restoring activities may need to be planned, to exemplify how necessary they are, as well as to discuss the necessity of finding ways to reduce the energy cost of large cluster activities such as school.

Lastly, if we examine a week schedule in calendar form, we may use colour coding as a way to keep an overview as well as potentially as a basis for gathering more information. Here we have simplified it slightly, but in several clinical cases, it has been useful to write out such a schedule hour by hour.

| | MONDAY | TUESDAY | WEDNESDAY | THURSDAY | FRIDAY | SATURDAY | SUNDAY |
|---|---|---|---|---|---|---|---|
| CRITICAL | | | | | | | |
| WARNING SIGNS | | DINNER | | | | | |
| | | SENSORY OVERLOAD | | | | | |
| | DINNER | | | | | | |
| | PLAYDATE | PLAYDATE | | | | | |
| | SCHOOL | SCHOOL | | | | | |
| | MORNING ROUTINE | MORNING ROUTINE | | | | | |
| | ANXIETY | ANXIETY | | | | | |

*Figure 7.2: Week schedule example*

This example is a slightly modified real-life example. Note that you could add more detail if you wished to do so, but that others may also prefer less detail.

| TIME | MONDAY | TUESDAY | WEDNESDAY | THURSDAY | FRIDAY | SATURDAY | SUNDAY |
|---|---|---|---|---|---|---|---|
| 6am | Morning routine | Morning routine | Morning routine | Morning routine | Morning routine | Morning routine | Morning routine |
| 7am | Leave house, transportation | Leave house, transportation | Leave house, transportation | Leave house, transportation | Leave house, transportation | Green time | Green time |
| 8am | Classes | Classes | Classes | Classes | Classes | Green time | Green time |
| 12pm | Lunch, quiet room Classes | Lunch, quiet room Classes | Lunch, quiet room Classes | Lunch, quiet room Classes | Lunch, quiet room Classes | Social time? | Social time? |
| 3pm | Classes | Transportation Homework | Classes | Classes | Transportation Homework | Social time? | Social time? |
| 5pm | Transportation | Green time | Transportation | Transportation | Green time | Social time? | Green time |
| 6pm | Dinner | Dinner | Dinner | Dinner | Dinner | Dinner | Dinner |
| 7pm | Homework | Green time | Homework | Homework | Green time | Social time? | Green time |
| 9pm | Evening routine | Evening routine | Evening routine | Evening routine | Evening routine | Evening routine | Evening routine |
| 10pm | Bedtime | Bedtime | Bedtime | Bedtime | Bedtime | Bedtime | Bedtime |

This is, of course, a schedule template for this person, meaning it does not include any changes that may occur from week to week. Rather, this is the general schedule for this person. You may note that many details that would be included in a Daily Energy Account Form are simply not included here – it would be far too much information.

What it does tell us is that, first, there are entire days which do not have any extended periods of time devoted to restoration. It also tells us that while there are many blue (physical health) activities, these are all regarding food and hygiene, not exercise. This would be something to explore.

Further, the differences in colour between the morning and evening routine reflect, for this person, that early mornings are difficult and stressful for them, whereas during the evening, they generally are able to relax a little more. Even though these two cluster activities will be similar in some ways, one is experienced as highly draining, whereas the other is not.

For this person, classes are marked as draining as well, due to the social and sensory aspects being very intense. However, once they are able to do their homework in a quiet and calm environment, this is a mental activity, not draining. This would be because the person does not find the academic work too challenging – but challenging enough to not be bored, as this might have made it a draining activity, too.

CHAPTER 8

# Guidelines for the Use of Energy Accounting

In this chapter of the book, we will outline an example set of 'rules' or guidelines that may be implemented when working with Energy Accounting. If you are using Energy Accounting with clients, either children or adults, it is important to remember to build these rules or guidelines according to the needs of each individual, and not to hold on to an example from this book as necessary to Energy Accounting as a method. The examples here are based on rules and guidelines put in place during previous casework, and, as such, they may be useful to others, but each person is different in what they find helpful. Always adjust to the individual.

As you use Energy Accounting, over time you will build a set of 'rules' that work for the individual. These rules will need to be adjusted according to the person's current state, meaning that if they are in a depressive or stressed period, certain rules may be beneficial to make changes to until they feel that they can return to the standard set of rules created for them.

## EXAMPLES OF 'RULES'
*Mental health day = no planned activity on this day, time for self-care and well-being activities*
Mental health days are often marked by crossing out the day in analogue calendars, and for virtual calendars it will be marked as an all-day event. For those using analogue calendars, as Maja

herself has done for many years, it may come to be known as 'x-ing out' a day. Tony experienced the value of a 'mental health' day when he worked for government agencies whose attitudes and policies he disagreed with and were a great drain on his energy reserves. The stress, frustration and energy depletion was not from working directly with clients but the policies, attitudes and bureaucracy of a government department. He could not resonate with the work culture and was at risk of developing burnout. As he looked through his diary and saw the number of policy meetings over the previous months and the number scheduled for the following week, he knew that he was at increasing risk of developing a sense of pessimism and lack of mental energy to achieve what he was required to do. He decided that he needed a 'mental health day' to restore the energy and commitment that he needed. The 'mental health day' was a day gardening and enjoying nature and being creative with plants.

Mental health days are primarily about removing sources of guilt, self-judgement and criticism. It does not work for everyone, especially those who get anxious when they have free time. However, for those who may have anxiety regarding living up to the expectations of completing tasks, or executive function challenges, it can be very helpful to schedule days where there are no expectations.

Often, these days are most effective when they are spent in solitude, but can work without complete solitude. If other people live with you or your client, it is important the other members of the household understand and respect that these days are in place to remove expectations and demands and to lower anxiety and stress. Because of this, they should not enter the person's room unless invited, and attempt not to initiate conversations unless necessary on those days. Most especially, these are days to avoid asking unnecessary questions and reminding the person of chores. There may be a 'Please do not disturb' sign on a bedroom door or a person may wear a T-shirt with the same message on the front.

It is important to note that these are not days when one *must* remain entirely inactive, but they are days when any activities are done due to genuine desire, not duty and responsibility.

We call these days 'mental health days', due to their importance in maintaining mental health. When people have the flu, they often take a day or a few days off to get better. We understand, as a society, that physical illness sometimes means you cannot work. In this same line of thinking, taking a day off – in the sense that you do not plan activity – when you are stressed, anxious or depressed, or indeed to prevent getting to that point, can give the mind the rest it needs to accelerate recovery or facilitate the prevention of mental health issues.

Note that these days are not necessarily weekdays, and can often be a weekend day that is purposefully kept clear of activity in order to make sure weekends do not contribute unnecessarily to stress. However, depending on the situation an individual is in, it may be necessary to take a mental health day off from school or work. These should be treated as any other sick day. It is not a case of 'skipping' school or work when this happens; rather, taking that day off is a necessary step in taking care of a person's mental health to study or work more efficiently in the long term. A supportive manager at work should ideally understand that sometimes people need a 'sick' day for mental rather than physical concerns. Alternatively, having part-time employment that allows for either longer weekends, with Fridays or Mondays off, or for Wednesdays off, providing a break in the middle of the week, can be highly beneficial. Maja herself finds most benefit from the mid-week break, whereas a friend of hers who is also autistic prefers to have Fridays off and have a longer weekend to decompress.

One significant point is that mental health days, while effective for many, can also be overused. A mental health day should not become a mental health month (unless you are on sick leave due to burnout, for example!), year or decade. What can happen for some is that mental health days are always spent inside and in solitude, which is perfectly okay – but not if this continues for too long. Many people report that after a week or a few weeks of staying inside, they can feel as though sensory and social experiences are much more intense and overwhelming on returning to social engagement. We know that if we do not have certain types of experiences for extended periods of time, there can be a feeling of having been sensitized to them, even if the experiences were okay before. This is to say, *for the sensory and social experiences that do not trigger sensory sensitivities*, regular exposure keeps the brain stimulated and helps it to learn to cope with the situations. When it falls 'out of practice', there is a period of relearning how to process the information within those situations.

By taking regular mental health days, we can hope to avoid a situation in which a mental health month, or even much longer, feels to the person like the only good option left.

## Filled square = 'more than normal'
For deposits and withdrawals, it may make sense to have a way to mark when the values are greater than normal. This could be marking an especially large social event, the first and/or last days of travel, first days of school following a holiday, or it could be having time to spend on a special interest when home alone!

On analogue calendars, this can be marked by drawing a square next to the name of the activity and filling it with colour. The size of the square may depend on how important it is to emphasize the event or activity. Some people also find a system by drawing the outline of a square, drawing a line through, a cross, or filling it in completely. Usually, this is something which develops, as the person needs a way to fill up their Energy Account in a more nuanced way.

Not everything is easy to implement in virtual calendars, and at first glance this is one of the difficult ones – however, there are many ways. For example, you can choose an emoji which has this meaning, or several which represent degrees of 'more than normal', as in the analogue example.

| | JANUARY | | | FEBRUARY | | | MARCH | |
|---|---|---|---|---|---|---|---|---|
| 1 | X | | 1 | X | | 1 | | |
| 2 | X | | 2 | ■ | Travel | 2 | | Doctor |
| 3 | X | | 3 | ■ | Travel | 3 | | |
| 4 | | School starts | 4 | | Travel | 4 | ■ | Help out friend |
| 5 | | | 5 | | Travel | 5 | X | |
| 6 | | | 6 | | Travel | 6 | | |
| 7 | | | 7 | | Travel | 7 | | |
| 8 | | | 8 | | Travel | 8 | ■ | Alone |
| 9 | | Dinner | 9 | ■ | Travel | 9 | ■ | Alone |
| 10 | | | 10 | X | | 10 | ■ | Alone |
| 11 | | | 11 | X | | 11 | | |
| 12 | | Doctor | 12 | X | | 12 | | |
| 13 | | | 13 | | Birthday | 13 | | |
| 14 | | | 14 | X | | 14 | | |
| 15 | | | 15 | X | | 15 | | |
| 16 | | Birthday | 16 | X | | 16 | | |
| 17 | X | | 17 | X | | 17 | | |
| 18 | | | 18 | X | | 18 | | |
| 19 | | | 19 | | Friend @ 11.00 | 19 | | Movie night |
| 20 | | | 20 | | | 20 | X | |
| 21 | | | 21 | | | 21 | | |
| 22 | | | 22 | ■ | Alone | 22 | | |
| 23 | ■ | Alone | 23 | | | 23 | | |
| 24 | | | 24 | | | 24 | | |
| 25 | | | 25 | | Visit friend @ 14.00 | 25 | | |
| 26 | | | 26 | | | 26 | | |
| 27 | ■ | Hairdresser | 27 | | | 27 | | |
| 28 | X | | 28 | | | 28 | | |
| 29 | X | | | | | 29 | | |
| 30 | | | | | | 30 | | |
| 31 | | | | | | 31 | | Dentist |

?  'MORE' (Draining/Relaxing, etc.)

X  MENTAL HEALTH DAY

*Figure 8.1: Calendar example*

The above example is a slightly modified real-life example from Maja's life many years ago. Certain information has been left out, like reoccurring school days and items that were otherwise part of normal routine. Note the large number of mental health days surrounding the travel.

In this particular case, Maja was close to burnout, but chose to go on a large family vacation anyway. In order to realistically avoid overload during the vacation, she had to take many precautions both before, during and after. Taking care to make sure her absence from school was not going to become a problem in the long run, she managed to schedule three mental health days shortly before the trip – again, these were not necessarily days of inactivity, but removing expectations and guilt. Having travelled before, she knew that the first few days would require additional energy in getting to know the place they were staying at, but also in coping with the reality of going through airports.

On returning home, she had planned to take one week of mental health days, but due to this being interrupted by a large social event, the mental health period had to be extended. However, this meant she was then able to return to school and a more regular schedule afterwards.

### No more than one major event per day
When first using the Energy Accounting approach, it is important to investigate what the value range of each activity is for you or your client. It will end up being different for each individual.

Cluster activities like school or work will often take up most of the day, and due to the social nature of most school and work environments, they can also take up most of the available energy for autistic people, introverts or others who find social environments difficult. For that reason, it is recommended in most cases to use this rule at first and later test if one's stress capacity allows for more activities in a day. Using this rule for the beginning of the process also allows for a more comfortable balance in which to investigate the costs and benefits of activities.

## One day off per week ('x-ed out')

As suggested earlier, it may be a good idea to begin with one mental health day per week, for example during the weekend. It allows for a day to catch one's breath during the process of investigating one's threshold, and is very often a part of maintaining a long-term balance in the schedule, especially for children.

## Draining activities should be balanced out as soon as possible

This is especially true for children. The ratio is hardly ever one to one in terms of time, but may still not be accomplishable if restoring activities such as special interests are only scheduled during the weekday evenings. If the person has several special interests, it may be good to leave the scheduling open, and writing 'special interest time', rather than any specific interest. If the person has a high need for structure, it will be the opposite, such that the specific interest is written in. Be sure to make time for all special interests, so that none are neglected, as this can be a stress factor by itself. However, this is a good start. If you feel comfortable with it, you may consider explaining the concept of Energy Accounting to a teacher, year coordinator or line manager, and the value of accessing energy deposit experiences during the school or work day.

Half or whole days for restoring activities may be needed occasionally, possibly often, depending on the person, their age, their ability to postpone needs, and their stress levels.

## At least one noticeable restoring activity per day

This holds true for almost any person at any age and stress level. An activity need not be a big deposit, nor time-consuming, in order to be noticeable and restoring. Adding little restoring activities to a day does not have to mean big, sweeping changes. It can be having a sensory toy such as a tangle or fidget spinner in a purse or pocket, available during either travel or breaks during the day. It can be having a five-minute meditation break once in a while. It can be taking a minute to look out of a window and just 'zone out'. Some people take advantage of having their smartphones with them by taking pictures of something that makes them smile or something they are grateful for such as their pet or collection of Lego models or a favorite book series. These little boosts make a difference even if you cannot find an hour or two for a restoring activity each day.

The important part of this rule/guideline is for the restoring activity to be something that the person is *conscious of* as a deposit, rather than 'something that just happens'. How we think about activities – the attention we give to them – can vastly change how we feel about them. So, taking a few minutes to zone out on purpose often has a greater effect than when we zone out without meaning to.

The trick, of course, is to figure out what the person needs in order to achieve well-being, and this may well mean continuously or habitually re-exploring this rule/guideline.

### Plan for alone time!
Certain people can be very dutiful and loyal towards others, sometimes to the extent that they will say yes to any invitation or request, regardless of whether or not they have the energy to do what they were asked. They can go overboard on postponing their own needs in such a way that it leads to stress and eventually depression or other psychiatric challenges. For this reason, it can be important to plan alone time to make sure the person gets time to themselves. It can be difficult for people who have this tendency to do this as they may feel selfish or as though they are letting others down. Such people may need a mantra for their alone-time days, such as 'The only person you need to be committed to is yourself' or 'This is not being selfish, it is a necessary survival mechanism'.

If someone needs support in being reminded that it is okay to need alone time, they can initially use their therapist for this; however, it often becomes most beneficial if a close friend or family member can take on this role. Furthermore, they may also work with the person in creating and rehearsing an explanation for needing time alone that is likely to be understood and accepted by teachers, colleagues or line managers. Alone time at work during breaks could be achieved by completing a crossword puzzle or reading a book, which are conspicuous signals to others to be left alone. Another option is going for a walk in a local park.

Some people stick to their own (immediate) needs of being alone regardless of the social or financial consequences. This can prompt them to skip school, work or social events. Often, this behaviour is made worse by their not knowing when they can next have time alone. Hence, by scheduling alone time, they know how long they have to cope with socializing, and may have an easier time postponing their need for solitude. However, in this case, it is vital to have the alone time scheduled at intervals the person can deal with, or it will not help. If the 'reward' is too far away, it does not help in the present.

## INTERACTING ENERGY ACCOUNTS

It should come as no surprise that people affect one another. By our moods and our actions, everything we do that involves other people affects them, and they affect us.

This means that people's energy accounts also affect one another. In our clinical work, we often work with families and this subject invariably comes up. A child will say that their parents' emotional state affects them, and the degree is often a surprise to the parents, as many children often do not fully verbally express this in the moment. However, when working with families, it is essential to examine how the child or children affect the parents and how the siblings or parents affect each other; very often, parents may need to be reminded that it is okay and very human indeed to be affected by their child's behaviour and emotional state. When working with parents of autistic children, it is valuable to examine and validate the energy cost for parents when their child has a meltdown or expresses suicidal ideation. The same applies to the partner of an autistic adult and the partner's energy cost.

Naturally, the energy cost for the autistic child or adult should never be ignored in this conversation, nor should the reasons for these symptoms to occur, but there is a cost for parents or a partner, too. This is crucial to examine when working with families, households or couples because it can increase their understanding of each other, as well as of themselves. Furthermore, it validates each person's experience without taking away from the experiences of others in the household. Most importantly, it leads to the conversation which many parents or partners do not often get to have with professionals: you are a better parent or partner when your stress levels are lower. The more we can balance the stress capacity and manage energy expenditure for the whole family, the better for everyone.

# PART 3

—— 𝕔𝕔𝕔 ——

# STAGES OF ENERGY ACCOUNTING

One could say there are two stages of Energy Accounting: one devoted to exploration, and one to implementation. This is not entirely true of course, as people never stop developing and, therefore, the exploration stage never *truly* ends.

However, in learning to use Energy Accounting, there is an initial period in which there is a markedly increased focus on 'detective work'. Usually, anywhere between two and six months will be spent in this initial exploration stage. In that time, a person spends time and energy devoted to self-exploration, as well as figuring out which parts of Energy Accounting work best for them. This time period is, for some, experienced as great relief in finally being allowed to express their needs and try living in a way they feel is more suitable for them. For others, the self-exploration is difficult, often due to being confronted with the ways in which they feel different from others. For this reason, it is often beneficial to have some therapeutic or other form of support during this time.

Once this initial period 'settles down', there is a sense of now being able to utilize Energy Accounting as a tool to keep track of and improve their lives. While it is still very possible to make mistakes and overburden themselves, or that unforeseen events still happen that cause consequences for the person's mental health and well-being, there is more often a sense of having tools available to cope with the situation in a structured and healthy way. This, then, is the implementation stage.

CHAPTER 9

# *The Exploration Stage*

The initial period of using Energy Accounting is spent exploring the person's life, getting a general overview, and identifying important factors. For exploration, we use the tools of Energy Accounting for self-discovery, and for doing 'detective work' in gathering information about energy expenditure and restoration.

It is expected that errors will be made during this process. The reason we state this so bluntly is that some may expect this process to be a steady progression towards improved well-being, and such an expectation would in most cases lead to disappointment. The fact is that people are complex, as are their lives, and the environments they live in. Many people with a range of diagnoses, including autism, may have co-morbid disorders (additional or co-existing diagnoses) such as an anxiety disorder, depression or ADHD, and experiences that may complicate a process such as this further. Because of this, any process that involves self-discovery, self-understanding and making changes to improve daily life is going to have that same complexity.

In the exploration stage, we expect to stumble on new information with some frequency, sometimes because a stress reaction such as a meltdown or anxiety attack is triggered when it was not expected. When this happens, we investigate what happened leading up to it, and make adjustments to the daily or weekly schedules accordingly. Likewise, when something works in creating emotional and energy stability and reserves, we do not merely continue doing it, but seek to understand why it works so that we can use it better. In short, we make an effort to learn from everything.

You will find a description of the therapeutic and clinical approach to the exploration stage in the clinical programme chapter, in Part 5 of the book.

## GENERAL OVERVIEW OF ENERGY VALUES

One of the first activities in the process is to form a general overview of the energy values of withdrawals and deposits, including their range. We often use a scale of 0–100, as this creates a systematic way to measure the varying 'strength' of these values. Numbers are recognizable and concrete, which makes them easier to work with for many people. If this does not work for any particular person, then use a different system. For those who prefer more simplicity, a 0–10 system, a metaphorical thermometer or barometer measuring temperature or pressure or a number of physical blocks representing the strength or 'weight' may work, with different coloured blocks for different sources of energy depletion or restoration. This may be in gradients of green-yellow-red, strong primary colours, or they may all be the same colour if different colours will be overwhelming for the person.

When speaking about the value of an activity, we begin by estimating a range. If the person is able to communicate either verbally or otherwise and able to aid in this process, their estimate is preferable as a starting point. These estimates may vary widely, even if – and sometimes especially – the activity occurs with high frequency. Sometimes, even with people who communicate easily, it can be useful to have input from close friends or family, as they may notice things the person themselves does not.

Activities that happen frequently are the ones to estimate first. In this regard, it can be helpful to use the Daily Energy Account Form to track activities for a week or two. Keep in mind that the activity of filling out this form will, in itself, have a cost. Some may find it enjoyable and informative, while others will find it dull or stressful.

It is not uncommon to see a combination of highly specific and surprisingly variable values; indeed this is often a sign of the person being engaged and reflective in the process.

An example of a source of energy depletion for an adolescent is noise in class which, let's say, has a range of 20–60. It is important to identify which noises cause more or less distress, and why. Knowing which sounds are involved, and their sources, can help in building strategies to better cope with the stressor. Furthermore, investigating the adolescent's acute stress reactions may be key in both helping them gain self-understanding, and knowing when to implement different strategies.

The range of a value estimate provides interesting and useful information that will help in structuring daily and weekly life at the 'template' level. We know that plans never quite work out, but having a sort of template to work from can be a great help, so long as the template feels manageable to the person. It can provide a sense of security in what to expect on a more general level.

With the estimates in hand, we can go about structuring a day and week that, in theory, should be 'safe' within the current budget. The day may be structured to alternate energy-depleting and -replenishing experiences.

Energy budgeting is based on anticipated expenditure. This prediction of expenditure can be reasonably accurate, but there may be a tendency to underestimate or even overestimate expenditure. With time and practice in using Energy Accounting, the predictions become more accurate and we become more likely to be able to 'balance the books' of withdrawals and deposits.

Note that all the information-gathering for Energy Accounting and the energy spent on working with Energy Accounting will have an energy cost which must be accommodated in the accounting system. Because of this, we advise that daily activities and responsibilities are scaled back at first. Think of it as cleaning, or tidying, the daily expectations. Things can be added back in later if it makes sense, but Energy Accounting should not be piled onto the already existing structure without making room for it. Usually, this will happen by itself, as Energy Accounting is introduced because the existing structure does not work, and it may quickly become plain that there are too few deposits during the day compared to expenses.

However, to achieve a balanced day or week template, we need further information and our exploration must continue.

## IDENTIFYING GENERAL STRESS THRESHOLDS AND PERIODIC FACTORS

In using Energy Accounting, some may seek to have their daily 'amount of available energy' represented by a simple number, such as 1000. This would mean that expenditures on activities would have to fall within this system or budget in order to be accepted. However, one of the keys to Energy Accounting is to understand that value differences represent the relative differences in costs between the activities and are not relative to the amount of energy available on a daily basis. This can seem like a strange distinction to make. However, for most users of Energy Accounting it tends to emerge that the daily maximum is not a set value but rather a dynamic one, changing in accordance with a great number of factors, or is much more difficult to pinpoint than working with cost estimates of activities.

The exploration stage is marked by attempting to identify a 'baseline' in the energy expenditure which is functional in the sense that frequent meltdowns or other stress symptoms may be avoided – this target will differ depending on the person, their age/maturity, history and other factors.

One way to get started is to begin by discussing 'good' days. What happened, what did not, which activities were completed, which were not? Which people were involved? Identifying patterns of such days can provide clues to a baseline for the acute stress thresholds. Think of it as a template.

Next, 'bad' days – what happened prior to meltdowns or other stress symptoms? Once again, this process is a matter of keeping track of activities and events over a period of time and identifying patterns. Some triggers may be obvious and can be noted quickly, others may take longer to spot. New ones may also emerge due to changes in age, maturity or daily routines.

A pattern may be identified of a meltdown being due to a significant depletion of energy from sensory and social experiences that have been relentlessly building throughout the day without any opportunity to achieve an energy deposit or release of tension. In other cases, we see stress reactions that are highly acute and situation dependent. These are often more difficult to avoid. Still, the self-exploration tends to pay off in the long term.

For the purposes of this exploration, we most often use the Daily Energy Account Form, and it can make sense to fill it out every day – or as often as the person remembers – for a week or two. Do not overcomplicate it with details; instead, focus on noting down the important parts of each day. In a sense, it is a diary, but focused on energy expenditure and restoration. This Daily Energy Account Form is also used for the next part of exploration, which focuses on important deposits and withdrawals.

We can use information from the Daily Energy Account Form, and patterns in stress symptoms, to get an idea of the person's stress capacity.

As we attempt to get an idea of a person's stress capacity, we also want to identify periodically reoccurring factors that will affect their stress capacity. This means we want to be conscious of when we should expect additional stress factors in the person's life. This includes external factors such as exams and holidays, but also internal factors such as pollen allergies, seasonal depressions, poor sleep or periods.

## IMPORTANT DEPOSITS AND WITHDRAWALS

Important deposits and withdrawals may emerge from a simple brainstorm, or they may take a while to pinpoint. When we speak about important deposits and withdrawals, we are referring to two primary 'categories' of activities or events:

- Those that occur frequently and can be predicted.
- Those that have consistently high values (in either direction).

For the initial exploration of deposits and withdrawals, it is important to decide first whether to write on paper or use a computer/ device. Due to the difficulties some autistic people have with handwriting – for example from fine motor skills or perfectionism – a computer or device may be preferred, but others may well prefer the freedom of handwriting, which allows doodling while thinking. They may also prefer to have another person writing for them. Depending on the person, this discussion or exploration can be very open, but simultaneously highly structured. The discussion should not veer off into a conversation about the hows and whys of the deposits and withdrawals, and certainly not in detail. As much as possible, stay on track to get things written down. There is plenty of time in the future to dive into details and explorations of self-understanding – and we do want this to happen, but first, we want to gather the important information.

If you are a professional working primarily with parents or carers, keep in mind that the results of the discussion should be regarded with flexibility and perceived as a provisional result. Because the person was not able to speak for themselves, their 'voice' or direct contribution is missing from the results. This does not mean the results of the discussion are not useful, it is simply something to keep in mind.

In the end, you should have a list of activities which can function as a reference when needed. The list may not need to be written down, but we do recommend it, and coming back to it to add new discoveries may be preferable, as many people tend to forget some activities because of the amount of information. Others have a great memory or develop something like an intuitive 'gut feeling' regarding this activity, and the list may not (continue to) be necessary.

## PRIMARY TRIGGERS FOR MELTDOWNS, ANXIETY ATTACKS AND SO ON

Each person has their own triggers which can take their anxiety or stress level from low to very high in a short period of time, sometimes just seconds.

For most people (if not all), persistently high stress levels will eventually result in some sort of meltdown or shutdown. If a person is in a stressful situation and cannot escape or have time to cool down, they will eventually react, potentially catastrophically.

● **SEE RESOURCE 8:** *Identifying Triggers for Negative Reactions.*

## IDENTIFYING PERSONAL STRESS AND WELL-BEING SYMPTOMS

This is a crucial part of exploration in Energy Accounting for all users. Knowing what our stress symptoms are is essential to monitoring our well-being, and our stress levels, as well as exploring our stress capacity.

Using a list of common symptoms is often beneficial as it helps us to think about just how many forms of stress symptoms there are. Well-being symptoms may be difficult to think of, as usually we may tend to think of the absence of stress symptoms. That is, a person may phrase a well-being symptom as 'feeling less anxious', or 'not feeling confused all the time'. We encourage a rephrasing of such descriptions whenever possible, but we do recognize this can be difficult and may be more easily accomplished much later in the process, as better self-understanding develops. Examples of stress symptoms and well-being symptoms can be found in the earlier chapters of this book and at EnergyAccounting.com/handouts.

Note that autistic people may sometimes need prompting or examples to recall their own experiences with these types of symptoms. Because they may experience high stress levels in general, their stress symptoms may be what they think of as their normal experience. It is very possible that when someone has been subjected to high levels of stress for a prolonged period of time, they cannot remember what not being stressed feels like. There are also issues of poor interoception at play. Interoception refers to the ability to sense the internal world, such as feeling hunger, temperature and physical discomfort, as well as perceiving heart rate, perspiration and muscle tension, which can indicate increasing levels of stress and agitation.

Furthermore, for people with impaired executive function, there will be symptoms that are commonly exacerbated by stress which are a part of their normal functioning. This, however, does not mean these symptoms will not worsen with stress. This includes poorer memory function, time perception and management, distractibility, and more. It is therefore important to keep in mind that a change in the degree of a symptom is relevant and should be included when discussing what stress and well-being look like for a person.

## PERSONAL COLOUR CODING

It will be during the first few conversations or sessions that colour coding can be introduced – again, depending on the person. Finding a personal colour-coding system can initially be a quick conversation. However, it may be changed at a later time if the initial system is inadequate or too complicated for that person's needs.

The chapter on colour coding in this book may be used as inspiration for where to begin.

When introducing colour coding, it will be important to remember that no colour category is seen as inherently positive or negative, even the one which represents recharging/restoring activities. There can be too many of any type of activity, even the deposits, if these activities mean there is not enough time left in the day to have the necessary amount of other types of activities, in order to have balance in the day. It is important to have diversity. If, for example, a person has filled their day(s) with special interest activities and forgets to eat or get enough sleep, this will negatively impact their mental and physical health. As such, the purpose of colour coding is not to identify 'good' and 'bad' activities, but to achieve an understanding of the balance of categories of activities that allows for personal well-being in a long-term perspective as well as in the short term.

The personal colour codes should reflect activities within the category that are not inherently good or bad, even if some of them are disliked. For this reason, it may not be preferable to include the least favourite colours in the coding. More importantly, the combination of colours should not trigger sensory sensitivities, and in this regard, taking a bit of time to find the colours and shades of those colours best suited for each person will likely pay off later. For some people, using very bright colours is preferable, whereas others feel much more comfortable using pastels.

## CREATING PERSONAL GUIDELINES

When creating the guidelines you will be using for your Energy Accounting, note that you must be prepared to be flexible and change them if they turn out not to work.

Often, the frequency of mental health days may be misjudged at first, and we suggest erring on the side of caution depending on the person you are working with. Autistic people can have a tendency to push themselves too far in an attempt to live up to others' or personal expectations, or wanting to be able to do what others can, such as being able to have social events every day following work or school. This often results in either acute meltdowns or longer-term consequences such as symptoms of stress, depression or autistic burnout, as well as seemingly random meltdowns which are the result of having been 'drained' over a longer period of time. Likewise, avoidance behaviours may appear or worsen as there is no mental energy available to engage in or initiate the requested action, or the action creates even further energy depletion.

Guidelines for how quickly draining activities should be balanced out are often based on the person's emotional maturity and ability to defer their needs to a later time. For some, it may have to be fairly immediate to counterbalance energy depletion; for others, a deficit on the account may be manageable for a few days or even a few weeks.

# CHAPTER 10

# *The Implementation Stage*

When the most intense parts of exploring are over and the person begins to feel confident in using Energy Accounting, we can begin to implement it in a strategic way in their daily life. Most often, this means having a daily and weekly routine that allows for unforeseen events to some degree, and being able to purposefully make changes to the routine whenever necessary.

A common example for young people is times of year when they have exams to complete. Energy Accounting is initially used to create a weekly schedule which works throughout the regular school weeks. However, once exams roll around, the schedule will need to be temporarily modified. Knowing that the person's stress capacity will be used more fully during some days means considering the weekly or even monthly planning and making changes to the activities that take place every day, in order to allow for the additional stressor of exam studying and completion.

There will be times throughout a person's life when, for a few days, a few weeks or a few months, they may need to spend more energy and live in a way that uses their full stress capacity. In the implementation of Energy Accounting, we do not expect to remove such time periods from people's lives. Rather, what we hope to do is create awareness for that person that, after such a time period, they will need time to recover. That is, they will need a time period when their stress capacity is respected to a greater degree, in which they can metaphorically 'pay off their energy debt' and save up again. This also means that monitoring well-being is a major part of implementing Energy Accounting successfully.

Energy Accounting does not remove the ups and downs of life, but aids in self-awareness, the monitoring of well-being, and the implementation of conscious, considered strategies for responding to stressors.

# PART 4

MAKING
ADJUSTMENTS

A big part of effective and realistic Energy Accounting is to make adjustments to the schedule template as needed. For people who are at school or otherwise have a steady and reliable schedule, it often makes sense to set aside a weekly 'appointment' for planning – what assignments need to be done this week, what are the priorities, which, if any, social events are there that the person is going to attend? For most people, it tends to be weekly or monthly schedules that are most necessary, with emphasis on any anticipated changes so that there are as few surprises as possible. For people with children, weekly planning and adjusting may not be enough, and we recommend checking up on how realistic the schedule is either twice a week or even every other day.

# CHAPTER 11

# *Adjusting to Systematic and Sudden Changes*

In the colour-coding chapter, we introduced the 'take care' category, used to mark times of year when a person's stress capacity is decreased. This is one way to keep track of systematic changes in stress capacity and is useful for taking into account certain types of stressors.

In this chapter, we will look at different types of systematic changes, and how we can adjust to them, using general examples. As always, remember to personalize Energy Accounting to the individual.

## SEASONAL DEPRESSIONS AND ALLERGIES

In colloquial terms, winter depressions may not necessarily be the type of depressions that require treatment, and for that reason, they can sometimes be perceived as 'not really serious' by many people. However, seasonal effects on mood are very real, and do negatively affect people's mental resources for that time period – in our terms, the stress capacity is lowered.

Pollen allergies can affect stress capacity as well, and, like seasonal depressions, can be predicted with some degree of accuracy. Allergies are in many cases easily medicated; however, the medication commonly leaves people feeling tired and flat. This can be viewed either as a primary stress factor which functions as a daily withdrawal, or as a lower capacity for activities during the duration. The result is the same. The overall amount of energy for each day is lower to one degree or another, depending on severity.

In both cases, no additional pressure from tasks or activities is required for the stress capacity to be lowered. Rather, the lower capacity stems from the body's reactions to seasonal changes. Seeing as we cannot change the seasons, the way to deal with such changes is to take them into account when planning.

## What to do

With the 'take care' category, you will be able to mark these time periods in advance, at least once you are aware of them. That means, if seasonal depressions are an issue, the goal will be to try to narrow down which factors are most causal – is it, for example, the temperature or the amount/intensity of daylight?

For instance, we might say that it is mainly the amount of daylight hours that contribute to the seasonal depression in a person who lives in northern Europe. The seasonal depression for this person tends to be most noticeable from mid-November to February. For each day during this time period, we can predict that there is less energy available to maintain the necessary activities for their life to run smoothly. This means that any non-essential activities need to be considered with regard to their contributions to the person's well-being, and whether it is a good idea to drop or cancel them (or maybe not plan too many in the first place).

A focal point for making any adjustment is an estimation of the change to the stress capacity. In essence: how significant a change do we have to make to usual planning strategies?

In the implementation stage, an estimation is made based on knowledge from the exploration stage. However, in the exploration stage, we expect to make more errors in this estimation. Depending on the age and support needs of the person you are working with, you should err on the side of caution and follow up with more frequent evaluations.

The estimation of the change to the stress capacity is used to reorganize any week-template you might have, as well as the day-to-day planning.

As an example, we might discuss a teenager with mild to moderate seasonal depression. For him, it is the winter darkness in Scandinavia which affects him the most, usually lasting three or four months from around November to February. It is possible that only minor changes to Energy Accounting may be needed overall. This may include adding vitamin D and calcium supplements, an additional half-hour or hour of sleep, emphasizing the exercise and healthy foods slightly, and decreasing social activity. Furthermore, emphasis can be made on outdoor activities during daylight hours, especially the middle of the day when the sun is highest.

However, due to the duration of this seasonal depression, these changes may still not be entirely sufficient in the long run. The case involves a teenager, and they may be able to handle a slight deficit in their budget for a few weeks (or one week) but certainly not a quarter of a year. Hence, we may need to reduce daily demands in favour of adding time for restoring activities.

● **SEE RESOURCE 9**: *Dealing with Infrequent Changes.*

## EXAM PERIODS, HOLIDAYS AND BIRTHDAYS
Generally speaking, there are often times of year that we associate with a higher or lower workload. Exam periods are one of these, for most people who are at school. For autistic people, holidays, with changes in daily routines, may be associated with the same feeling but the source of increased workload instead has to do in large part with the increased intensity of social interaction – and thus, increased amounts of energy spent on analysing and processing social information. Holidays can also be a sensitive period for many people, including autistic people, for the opposite reason: loneliness. This is a different kind of strain, and our way of coping with it through Energy Accounting would be different as

well. Instead of decreasing the workload in other areas, we might instead seek to increase various forms of social interaction in ways that are possible with the framework and resources in that person's life. This might involve increased contact with online friends and acquaintances, creating contact with groups that engage in shared interests, or it may be volunteering in some capacity that provides social contact. Likewise, we may also seek to distract a little from the loneliness by planning activities around interests or skills. This might be a project to write or create something, going out to somewhere connected with the interest, or setting aside time in the day to work on or seek information regarding a skill or topic the person finds energizing. A combination of the two approaches may well be advised.

Let us discuss an example of a person who has a hard time with additional social activity during Christmas as well as the sensory environment, and begins to feel anxious about the festive time a month in advance because they know how overwhelming it will be. They may not feel they can say no to attending family gatherings, or even to going home early from them.

We would want to decrease social and sensory pressure leading up to the holiday as much as possible. This could include ordering presents online rather than going to physical shops, taking a mental health day off work/school before the social event, and perhaps two or three afterwards, if at all possible. We would also seek to give the person strategies to alleviate the stress during the social gathering, such as taking a 'bathroom break' to get a few minutes of quiet, or stepping outside for some air, doing a few breathing exercises, or perhaps arriving early when there are fewer family members present and so it is easier to cope with in terms of energy depletion, and it may feel more accepted to leave early. In time, we would prefer the family to receive some psychoeducation so they can help implement strategies to make it easier for the person to attend the Christmas celebrations – this could involve having a quiet room, making it easy for the person to leave earlier than others or to only take part in the portion of the celebration they feel most comfortable with, and having sensory shielding such as noise-cancelling headphones available at the dinner table.

Another person feels lonely during holidays. For whatever reason, they either do not have contact with their family, or they do not get together often or celebrate specific dates and events. They are easily overwhelmed by social and sensory information and thus cannot volunteer somewhere, as this often causes meltdowns or anxiety attacks. The friends they usually socialize with online have celebrations to go to and are unlikely to be available.

We can focus on socializing via text online in the form of messages of gratitude or well-wishes for the holidays, hopefully getting some in return. If the person is interested in online games there are likely some people online in most multiplayer games. We can also increase time spent on the special interest, setting an achievable but difficult goal, such that they are occupied for the day or a few days by it. By planning in advance, we may be able to increase social time slightly in the following few days, and then return to normal amounts of socializing.

● **SEE RESOURCE 10**: *Focus on Exams.*

Holidays and birthdays may require days off, often preferably alone days, before and after the events. How many days depends on the person, and on the amount of social time, and the number of people involved. It is also important to consider the following factors:

- Is there someone present who is particularly energy-draining?
- Do the people present know about and accept the person's need to be alone, or to have quiet time?
- Are there particular sensory difficulties involved which it is difficult to plan around?

The examples regarding holiday adjustments can serve as

inspiration for adjustments that may work for you or the person you are working with. Remember to take into account any prior or looming anxiety and to plan restoring activities and mental health days to recover afterwards.

## SLEEP

● **SEE RESOURCE 11:** *Focus on Sleep.*

We know that some people have sleep problems that are cyclical in nature. We can think of this as a systematic change that we can adjust to. For some people, the pattern is monthly, moving in accordance with hormonal changes, and some report being affected by the lunar cycle. For others, there are problems with sleep that is affected by the season, or by weather. We can use self-monitoring tools such as those employed in a mood diary, scoring sleep on one or more factors over time, and noting any particular cyclical information.

When a pattern is identified, we can be pre-emptive in introducing strategies or lowering expectations. Remember that most strategies take a while to implement as there is an initial adjustment period where we may not be sure if it will work or not. Sometimes we can know immediately that a strategy is successful or entirely wrong for that person, but for the most part, we should allow up to three months of using a strategy before we evaluate it.

## CHANGES IN MEDICATION

Another change which we can anticipate, to some degree, is a change in medication. It could be a change in dosage, in the type of medication, or within a specified range of medications for a particular therapeutic indication, such as a different medication to treat anxiety, depression, or ADHD, or a hormonal birth control. Each of these medications will have different potential side effects.

Whenever we alter medications or dosages, we can expect some degree of changes in the medication's effect, side effects, or both – or to put it another way, the positive and negative impact the medication has on the person's life. With such changes in effect and side effects, there is often a period of physical and psychological adaptation, which for some people can be a few days, and for others can be a few weeks or even months. While we always hope that the new medication will create a physical and psychological improvement and no worsening in side effects, it is sensible to prepare for potential changes and to seek advice from the prescribing physician on the primary effects and side effects of any changes in medication.

We recommend preparing for at least two weeks during which demands need to be lower, and rest time increased. If this turns out to be unnecessary, the additional rest time can be reduced faster than initially planned, and demands can be increased again.

## ADJUSTING TO SUDDEN CHANGES

Sudden, unanticipated changes to plans occur (almost) every day. It can be an alarm that does not go off or does not wake you, sudden illness, traffic congestion, or an unexpected or unwanted phone call. So many things can push a schedule or planned activity outside our control, and when this happens, most people adjust automatically, changing their plans in a way they find acceptable, but during times of stress it becomes more difficult to make adjustments on the fly. Once the unexpected event or crisis is over, it is important to recognize the degree of energy depletion in adjusting to the sudden change, and to make appropriate adjustments to the energy account as soon as possible.

Sudden changes are not always situational, however. Sometimes, a sudden change can mean making adjustments for several days, weeks or months.

## LATENT REACTIONS

In some people, cognitive processing time is increased. This means that any or all types of information may take longer to cognitively process. Commonly, and especially for autistic people, emotions take longer to cognitively process – this means also that emotions can sometimes be expressed hours, days, weeks or months after the event that caused them occurred. It is also relatively common that emotions are not fully processed the first time around and, after some time, need to be reprocessed.

We see this especially in children who are going through school refusal. There can be an initial burnout, usually taking a few months, wherein there is loss of skills, and cognitive functions are affected. Then, there seems to be improvement for a few weeks or months, and then suddenly, as if out of nowhere, the improvement disappears and there is a new period marked by loss of skills, refusal towards everything, and other reactions to stress or trauma. One way of viewing it could be that the child's nervous system was not able to fully process the stress all at the same time, and has to process the experiences and emotions several times over before it can effectively repair itself.

With such long-term reactions, long-term adjustments must also be made. It will often take some time to recognize that this is what is happening, but once recognized, the latent reaction should be treated as burnout.

Latent reactions can also occur with shorter delay, and with smaller reactions. For example, a child may attend a birthday party – let us say on a Friday – and have a great time there, enjoying the socializing, games and food. Because the child is so happy and not apparently energy depleted from the event, parents or carers may assume the child will be fine. In many cases, there will be a reaction the following day, with marked tiredness, inability to cope with new information or experiences, and potentially emotional outbursts. However, in some cases, the child appears not to react for several days and it may not be until Monday that their reaction occurs. They may therefore need a day or two off school to recover, and otherwise certainly should be offered additional restoring activities for a few days. Moreover, the information gathered from the latent reaction should be used to plan for restoring, calming activities before and after future social events similar to that party. Some carers and professionals may be inclined to say 'the birthday party was obviously too much, and we should not do that again', but if the child truly enjoyed the party and wants to go to similar events, there is no reason to keep them from doing so – remember, our criticism of the resilience approach only applies to experiences that are potentially traumatic, such as extreme adverse sensory experiences. We all learn that we are capable of coping with situations by being challenged – just enough, but not too much. It may be that the next few birthday parties should be followed by a mental health day, or the child may prefer to be at the party for a shorter duration next time.

Use the information gained to make guidelines for how to adjust in the future.

# CHAPTER 12

## *Burnout*

Burnout is increasingly recognized as a response to long-term stress in adults. Initially, job burnout was the primary topic, after which parental burnout became a focus for some researchers. Unfortunately, not many people, even professionals, at this time recognize school burnout in children or adolescents, or social and sensory causes of burnout.

Clinically, we increasingly see children and adolescents who have been coping with the pressures they face in life in general, but especially in school, and who end up in burnout. The symptoms are similar to those of adults. Most often, there is loss of cognitive functions, affecting the ability to learn and recall information, emotion regulating is impaired, and there are social and behavioural symptoms, often including withdrawal. School refusal is a very common symptom for children and adolescents in burnout, but some will attempt to continue attending school even when burnout has begun. In such cases, stress reactions such as meltdowns and shutdowns tend to increase in frequency and often severity, grades may go down rapidly and teachers may report experiencing an entirely different child.

We know from job burnout that recovery takes anywhere from a few months to approximately one and a half years and involves long-term sick leave and a slow, gradual return to work. As we suspect based on the research that underlies adverse childhood experiences, children's nervous systems may respond differently to frequent, prolonged or strong stressors and it is possible that cortisol causes more damage to their nervous systems (Burke Harris 2018).

Based on this, children could take longer to recover from burnout, or their recovery process may be different in other ways. However, the primary intervention – or treatment – is the same as for adults. A combination of a varied and healthy diet, regular (moderate) exercise, getting enough quality sleep, having a sense of community, and touch that the child feels good about receiving or giving (do not force children to hug people they do not want to hug), are all key to the treatment of burnout, just as with other forms of long-term stress.

Once symptoms of burnout show themselves and are recognized as such, we often need to adjust very quickly and make sweeping changes to daily life. We begin by removing as many demands as possible, and providing access to calming and pleasant experiences, along with plenty of rest. One category of activities we would not recommend scaling back on is basic physical health activities – that is, hygiene and diet. Exercise may need to be altered to suit the current state of the person, in that they may need a period of indoor exercise or lower intensity exercise. Another category of activities for recovery from burnout is time in nature and with animals. There may also need to be psychological support for the consequences on self-esteem and other aspects of mental health.

Any demands that are added back into their lives should be done so in a planned, controlled way, with some monitoring, preferably both self-monitoring and observations by others. We frequently see that a child or adolescent will jump back into activities without regard for increasing stress symptoms, or hold back from activities to a degree that becomes harmful. They may need help to regulate the amount and types of activities that are added.

Use the information gathered during this process to plan for the future. Do an investigation to find out what led to burnout, such that it can be avoided in the future. The goal is to create a daily life that is functional and desirable for the individual.

For autistic people, there is the potential for great stress and chronic exhaustion from trying to cope with social and sensory experiences, being misunderstood and criticized, having high levels of anxiety and, for many reasons, not feeling in touch with or being able to express their authentic self. In addition, there may be self-imposed expectations that are greater than coping mechanisms and current capacity. Subsequent stress can build up over time and lead to autistic burnout. In a sense, the frontal lobes in the brain are 'closed', awaiting recovery. A major cause of autistic burnout is being in a non-autism-friendly environment with attitudes and expectations that cause considerable chronic stress.

## SIGNS OF AUTISTIC BURNOUT

The concept of autistic burnout has come from autobiographies, internet support groups and clinical experience. There are provisional criteria for autistic burnout, according to Higgins *et al.* (2021):

- Significant mental and physical exhaustion.
- Interpersonal withdrawal.

There is often one or more of the following:

- Significant reduction in social, occupational, educational, academic, behavioural or other important areas of functioning.
- Confusion, difficulties with executive function and/or dissociative states.
- Increased intensity of autistic traits and/or reduced capacity to camouflage/mask autistic characteristics.

There can also be associated features:

- Low self-esteem and not knowing what to do to restore mental energy levels.
- Confusion as to whether the signs are indicative of a clinical depression.

- Loss of self-care skills and ability to regulate emotions.
- Persistent difficulties with daily living skills.

When considering whether someone has autistic burnout, it is important to review the similarities and differences between autistic burnout and depression. In comparison to the signs of depression, in autistic burnout there is increased sensory sensitivity and the need to isolate in order to recover. The current clinical and experiential wisdom is that autistic burnout is a cause of depression, and that the depression is likely to reduce if measures are taken to resolve the causes of autistic burnout.

## CAUSES OF AUTISTIC BURNOUT

- A lack of autism awareness and accommodations at school, work, within the family, government agencies and society.
- Feelings of being judged negatively and rejected.
- Being perceived as defective.
- A lack of progress academically or at work.
- More demands at school, work or home than coping abilities.
- A lack of connection and relationships with others.
- Diminishing mental energy and increasing stress and self-doubt.
- Camouflaging autism and/or mental health issues.

Autistic burnouts can last months or years and may start in the adolescent years. A burnout may be triggered by life changes such as leaving school, starting a new job or promotion, or the end of a friendship or relationship. The experience of burnout may precede and precipitate a diagnosis of autism, and confirmation of the diagnosis may lead to the recognition of autistic burnout.

Burnout is more likely for autistic adults who camouflage and suppress their autism. Unfortunately, there can be a tendency to not communicate their true support needs and level of exhaustion and valiantly try to cope at school or work. However, the cost of this camouflaging, or masking, is that emotional and cognitive energy depletion contributes to burnout. Camouflaging becomes a barrier to support and relief, and increases stress, even though the person may have seen it as a strategy for survival.

## RECOVERY FROM AUTISTIC BURNOUT

The first stage is recognizing being in a state of burnout. It is a process that requires self-awareness and being prepared and able to disclose the fatigue, stress and despair. Those who know the autistic person well may perceive the signs of burnout before the autistic person does. This can be due to difficulties with interoception and denial.

There may need to be guidance and support in becoming a self-advocate and explaining to those at school or work the daily challenges experienced by an autistic person and the accommodations and adjustments needed to reduce stress and recover from autistic burnout.

Empathy and practical suggestions may be obtained from the autistic online community. The greatest expertise is with those who have themselves experienced autistic burnout.

The autistic person's current expectations, lifestyle and supportive environment need to be reviewed with a stress assessment to determine which aspects of their life can be 'pruned' to help restore energy levels. This may include changing employer, career and lifestyle. A psychologist or therapist can help determine what depletes and what restores energy levels. Treatment for autistic burnout is, in many ways, the same approach that is used for other forms of burnout or long-term stress. However, there also needs to be a focus on encouragement to be their authentic self and explain rather than inhibit autistic characteristics.

As clinicians, we have a few words of caution regarding the value and effectiveness of traditional cognitive behaviour therapy (CBT) and behavioural activation as an automatic choice of therapy for an autistic burnout and associated depression. The genuine need for withdrawal and downtime (avoidance) for recovery may be contrary to the central themes of CBT, and the characteristic of reduced cognitive capacity may inhibit the effectiveness of these therapies. That is, these forms of therapy would need to be adjusted to the autistic individual, according to the latest knowledge on autism. It will be crucial that a therapist has the knowledge and ability to make these adjustments.

## DEADLINES AND PRIORITIES

As much as Energy Accounting is an attempt to plan when and how our energy should be spent, plans tend to go wrong when faced with reality. Because plans tend to change, it is often important to know how to best prioritize our time and the tasks at hand.

For instance, a homework, university or work assignment may be due on a certain day, and reserving enough energy resources to complete that may be prioritized over, for example, certain recreational activities or socializing. However, this can only be done to a certain extent before it will have mental health consequences.

So, a deadline will be marked on the calendar as an event, as well as planning when the assignment is scheduled to be written, and a priority can be set for that activity. Likewise, activities that are scheduled, but may be moved, can have a marker for their priority setting. Each individual may have a preferred way to mark priorities, and they often take different forms depending on the person's scheduling tool – a physical calendar, a phone app or a web app. For a phone or web app, certain emojis can be chosen to represent degrees of importance or priority, or it could be symbols that are chosen. For a physical paper calendar, it could be one or more types of symbol but in different colours.

Generally, we do see that using the exclamation marks can have downsides. When highlighting things with one, two or three exclamation marks, many people can give themselves additional stress, as this symbol tends to indicate urgency and severity in a way that may not be intended here. Instead, we are looking for a way to communicate the information that is a priority, rather than to cause any anxiety or stress.

If a person finds the amount of information confusing or stressful, do not hesitate to discontinue the use of priority marking for activities.

Using these deadlines and priorities in a calendar can be helpful when needing to adjust to any sudden changes, as there will be an overview of things that cannot be moved – and thus have higher priority – as well as other activities. We can then move things around as possible, and ask others for help with certain aspects if necessary.

When marking deadlines and priorities, and indeed when planning any amount of time ahead, remember to be realistic about how many useful hours this person has in a day. People are very different, not only based on temperament or personality, but most definitely on age, maturity and, not least, disability. Some people may have ten or twelve "useful" hours in a day, and others may have only two hours. People with certain conditions may have a highly unstable number of "useful" hours per day, some days having no mentionable "useful" time at all, and other days being highly productive, perhaps even to a level that others find unachievable.

The amount of time a person has to reasonably do things in a day or a week is always limited, and their limit should be taken into account and respected at all times. Most often, people may expect more of themselves than is realistic, and they may need support in lowering their expectations to a realistic level and, as we say, forgiving themselves for being human.

We have found that a common characteristic of autism is having unrealistically high expectations of personal abilities and achievements – including recognizing the number of useful hours in a day. These are often greater than expected by a parent, teacher, colleague or line manager. There is a determination to seek perfection, and sometimes perfection is not required. Because of this, there may be a greater need to have other people help in managing these expectations. It can be very useful indeed to do weekly planning with another person who can step in to remind the autistic person not to expect too much of themselves and to be a reality check in terms of what other people can reasonably do, and what is likely to be the actual expectation from teachers, managers or colleagues – precisely because it is often much lower than the autistic person believes it to be.

● **SEE RESOURCE 12**: *Adjusting to Changes with Age.*

# PART 5

————— ◀◀◀◀◀◀ ————

# CLINICAL IMPLEMENTATION

When implementing Energy Accounting as a clinician, you can use the clinical programme provided, but do not feel that this is the only approach – it is merely what we recommend, especially as you are getting to know the method better.

As the method is so highly visual, we recommend working either on paper sheets which the client can bring home, on a whiteboard, or on giant post-its. You or your client can also take a photograph of the whiteboard or giant post-it on a mobile phone as another record of the information. Whenever possible, finding ways to visualize the process tends to work well with autistic people or others who are visual thinkers.

It is often beneficial to include a carer, close relative, partner or friend in one or more sessions. First, they may have observations to share which can be illuminating and which the person may forget to bring up or not realize themselves. Second, they may learn something about the client's experience which will give them a different perspective and help them in supporting the client. There can indeed be a greater degree of compassion stemming from the insight a person gains about the client by participating in the programme. Another advantage is that parent/carer/relative/friend may subsequently remind or prompt your client to use an Energy

Accounting analysis or strategy and provide encouragement and positive feedback when implementing Energy Accounting.

They may not have to participate in every session, and we recommend that this is discussed with the client and the person they have brought during the first or second session. The client's opinion should be taken into account, but the benefits should be explained. Whenever possible, we recommend that someone close to the person participates at least twice during the programme – especially during the Energy Bank discussion, and session on monitoring well-being.

It will be important that your client is informed of any rules or laws of confidentiality in your profession and country. They must understand that including anyone and specific events in their Energy Accounting programme is entirely their choice and that this choice will be respected. This means sharing information with parents, carers, schools or anyone else regarding their Energy Accounting and support needs is something you will only do if they want this to happen. This information should be given at the beginning of the first appointment, so as to leave no doubt.

# CHAPTER 13

# Clinical Programme Outline

This outline is meant to simply be one suggestion for how to approach a clinical session programme. Each person will need personal modifications, and our primary advice is to always individualize as much as possible. The more you have worked with Energy Accounting, the more you will be able to juggle the tools and concepts and adapt to each person as needed, and for this reason, we suggest that clinicians and carers try Energy Accounting out among their colleagues or with a friend or family member first, to gain familiarity. We also suggest that you try it out with yourself, in order to gain personal experience which may help you relate to how the client feels when you introduce Energy Accounting activities with them. You will be able to tell them, authentically, that you have tried this and understand why it may seem confusing or perhaps overwhelming at times. The concept of Energy Accounting could be introduced with your personal example and how Energy Accounting is incorporated in your life, or with a case you have worked with before. The introduction to the components is then not unique to the autistic person and they can learn 'the rules of the game' without feeling they are the focus of the activity.

However, once they are comfortable with Energy Accounting, it is time to make it as personal and customized as possible. Relate it to their everyday experience, make it concrete and approachable. For some people, this means removing much of the weird theory or neuro talk, whereas for others, understanding this part is what makes Energy Accounting seem sensible. Be prepared to mix and match to fit the person's needs and interests, and continue to check in with them if things make sense, are interesting, or seem useful right now. Sometimes, we find that an idea introduced weeks or months ago suddenly makes sense to a person, and then they want to work with it, even though they did not before. Be prepared, as with all other clinical work, to stay 'on your feet'.

Try not to make things too serious. Be relaxed and collaborative. Very often, clients are uncomfortable with the novelty of Energy Accounting, and if you are light-hearted about it, and do not seem to be 'hung up' on things, the person can sometimes feel more at ease. This also means that the approach to using Energy Accounting in a clinical setting should be one that focuses on making it as relaxed and fun as possible for the person, while making it relevant. Again, they may or may not want to feel as if their own experience is the focus, so keep in mind to ask and make adjustments.

Lastly, consider timing and pacing. Each person will be different in how often they want a session, or how quickly they can cope with adding new information or approaches. If a person is already highly stressed or distressed, having too frequent sessions, or indeed not frequent enough, adding homework or new elements too quickly can become a stress factor instead of a positive experience.

You may take inspiration from feedback-informed treatment approaches, encouraging your client to evaluate each session and critique your approach such that you may better adapt to their needs.

Note that this clinical programme outline, while divided into eight stages, is likely to take a different number of sessions for each stage, depending on each person. Some people will need to spend a longer or shorter time on some topics. Furthermore, when discussing a session programme at the very beginning, do recommend having between one and three sessions after the end of the primary programme dedicated to evaluation and follow-up. These sessions may be spread out over a relatively long period of time, allowing for follow-up as the client encounters new challenges or is ready to learn additional strategies to add to their 'toolbox'.

## STAGE 1: BRAINSTORM DEPOSITS AND WITHDRAWALS

Stage 1 focuses on:

- intake evaluation and discussion
- introducing Energy Accounting
- discussing deposits and withdrawals
- brainstorming to promote greater self-understanding.

### *Intake evaluation and discussion*

In the first session, there are a number of points to go through, as with any clinical programme.

Naturally, introductions need to be made, and both you and the client need to figure out during the session whether you are a good match – whether you get along, in essence. We are never the right clinician for every single client we meet, and this is natural and normal. Likewise, it might make sense to let the client know that if this is the case, there will be other clinicians who may be a better match for them, who can still help them through this programme. Basically, make the point, 'You can still get help. I am not the only clinician who could have helped you.' If needed, do aid them in finding an alternative clinician.

It may also make sense to do a clinical evaluation, for example using the Depression, Anxiety and Stress Scale (DASS). This could be repeated at the end of the programme if both you and the client feel this would be beneficial. For the intake evaluation, the DASS can give you an indication of the severity of existing depression, anxiety and stress. If you have another preferred screening tool, do use this as it is important that you are comfortable and familiar with the methods you are using.

Discuss with the client the results of the intake evaluation, and how you both would like to begin the programme. This may include details of their life you should be especially attentive to, or prior experience with therapy which may or may not have been positive.

### Introducing Energy Accounting
Here, you could take inspiration from Chapter 1, What is Energy Accounting?

When presenting Energy Accounting to your client, you can include the following points:

- This will not fix everything, it is not a magic cure for stress, no such thing exists. However, this is an approach that can help you *understand your stressors, inspire changes, help to build resilience against future stress and improve your quality of life*. (Include this point only in order to manage expectations. We want to be realistic about what can be done.)
- We will be able to see in one to four months if each strategy we try out works or not, so it is important to have patience.
- There are lots of little ways to approach the challenges associated with stress. Not everything works for everyone, and that is okay. We are just going to try to figure out what works for you. We are going through the 'toolbox' of ways to handle the challenges associated with stress and improving your quality of life. Whatever we find out works for you is great, and that is what we will build on going forward.

Briefly present the concept that everyday experiences and activities cost energy and give energy – if the client is already on board with this concept, do not spend more time on it than necessary. You will likely have more success if you begin with exploring emotions, interoception and recognizing stress symptoms.

### Discussing deposits and withdrawals
People are vastly different in how easy it is to put into words what drains them of energy or refreshes energy. It is often beneficial

to use lists of activities included in this book for inspiration, even for those who can name energy deposits and withdrawals by themselves, as there may be additions to the lists they had not considered before. As you gain experience with the application of Energy Accounting with your clients, you will increase your list of potential energy deposits and withdrawals and identify possible patterns and variations due to age, gender, experiences and additional diagnoses. Because of this, you will be better able to aid with suggestions.

Start by making a deposits and withdrawals list, without necessarily assigning value ranges to each activity – that can come later. At the beginning, it is often useful to focus on deposits and withdrawals that are likely to have higher value ranges, but sometimes this is not possible or not useful for the client. This is especially true for those who may not feel they have any – or enough – good deposits of energy to mention.

Try to make sure there are more deposits than withdrawals, even though this may be incredibly difficult for some people. Withdrawals tend to be easier to name, especially for people who are depressed, anxious or have been stressed for a prolonged period of time. If the person cannot think of more things to put on the deposit or withdrawal side, you may make suggestions, from your knowledge of the client, or suggestions from this book, but do not pressure the person to add to the list. It may take a while for them to process everything, and after a few days (or weeks) of mulling over the list of suggestions, they may suddenly recognize deposits or withdrawals that are relevant to them.

If the person has brought a carer, relative, partner or friend with them, they may help with these lists of withdrawals and deposits. Often, they are especially helpful with contributing ideas for deposits. Furthermore, as mentioned earlier in the Energy Bank chapter of the book, creating these lists can be an eye-opener and a reality check for both the client and anyone they have brought with them. This is often a positive experience, but can also be overwhelming. Be sure to stay mindful of how this is impacting your client and help them to manage any negative emotional reactions, such as shock, hopelessness or shame. Remind them that as they go through the process involved in Energy Accounting, they will learn more information and new ways to manage stressors in their life, even if it can seem daunting. They may very well feel as if they are standing at the bottom of a self-discovery mountain, awaiting a tough climb. In reality, the journey tends to become easier over time, rather than harder, and you are a mountain guide that is familiar with the best routes to use when climbing the mountain.

Once a list is created, you can begin assigning value ranges to activities. How much does socializing cost? Socializing with friends, family, even with specific people or under specific circumstances, may have different costs; thus the cost is put as a range, as noted throughout the book. At a later stage of the programme, socializing can easily be subdivided into different people, groups of people and social situations and examined in more depth. However, if the person wants to do this right away, it can be beneficial to follow them in their interest and enthusiasm.

### Brainstorming to promote greater self-understanding

Understanding why activities have the effect on your energy they do is key to being able to adjust plans, find ways to strengthen deposits and diminish withdrawals, and advocate for yourself in certain situations. This is an aspect where Energy Accounting goes further than mere stress management and can be used to enhance quality of life through self-understanding. However, remember that not everyone is ready to talk about why things are the way they are, either due to their capacity to handle stressors at the time, or perhaps due to age, maturity, cognitive abilities or challenges with depression. Adjust to their current capacity and needs.

You, with your client's input, may begin by choosing one deposit or withdrawal to explore, by asking questions about the activity. For example, many adults have an ongoing to-do list in their minds. Having a mental to-do list would be neutral if there were no emotions or reactions to thoughts about it – having *guilt* about not achieving the things on the list, or feeling overwhelmed by it, explains why it costs energy. The list itself may well not be a problem.

As another example, an autistic teenager enjoys walking their dog. When asked, they might explain that their dog is the easiest one to socialize with in their household. But we know there are definitely other aspects of dog-walking that are positive. These include: being outside, especially in sunlight, walking (movement in general), and having one specific task to focus on, clearing the mind from having to make choices or analyse other information. On discussing this, we may find out that this teenager actually prefers walking around dusk, because sunlight is harsh to their eyes. They also say that walking the dog is sometimes better than playing with the dog at home, because they are not interrupted while walking. This gives us several clues regarding stressors that may apply elsewhere: visual sensory sensitivity, and social or cognitive sensitivity to being interrupted during a task.

The results of the discussion will be informative and illuminating for all participants. It is important not to be judgemental or to dismiss your client's suggestions, but you may seek further clarification or examples in their daily life.

One aspect that is frequently beneficial to discuss is that of structure and consistency versus flexibility and options. A more concrete example of this might be the morning routine. Some people find it comforting to know that their morning routine is exactly the same every single day, while for others, this is actually stressful. However, too much 'freedom' can be a stress factor as well. If you have no idea what you are going to wear that day, some people will feel comfortable just 'throwing something on' and heading out, whereas others will have a meltdown or anxiety attack because it will take too long to decide in the morning. Such factors in each person's personality will be an important part of the self-discovery process in Energy Accounting.

If the conversation seems to stall, it may be useful to maintain momentum by discussing the following points:

- How to strengthen some of these deposits or lessen the withdrawals, suggesting strategies for coping with sensory, social or other challenges.
- Identifying *one* useful rule/guideline to try out. Begin with one, to limit the number of changes made at once. This is both because it will then be easier to figure out what is helping and what is not, and because making too many changes at once can be overwhelming and decreases the chance that the person will keep up the changes.
- Psychoeducation, if there is something relatively quick that is highly relevant to the conversation you have already had. This can include brief examples, such as how a great deal of mental energy is consumed by managing anxiety, and playing computer games can be a fast and efficient means of energy deposit.

It may also be useful to include/spend a few minutes discussing these points:

- Stress is a normal, human response. It does not mean you are weak, just that your environment did not match your needs or abilities at the time.
- The brain does heal itself when it is allowed the 'space' to do it.

Close the session or stage by making suggestions for what you might do next time – the client will be able to respond and you can gauge their openness towards parts of the method. Furthermore, this will prepare them for future topics such that it is easier to begin working with some of these when the time comes. Any preferences they may have for where to continue will be helpful in them getting a sense of ownership of the process.

## STAGE 2: INTRODUCE DIFFERENT ACCOUNTS AND COLOUR CODING
Stage 2 focuses on:

- beginning evaluation
- introducing accounts and colour coding
- follow-up on deposits and withdrawals lists
- making one change based on the conversations so far.

### Beginning evaluation
From this point onwards, we want to begin to introduce evaluations with the client. We start with a narrower focus, as there are not yet many aspects of Energy Accounting that have been introduced.

For now, spend a few minutes asking the client whether they have given any thought to the discussions from last time, and if so, what these have been. Perhaps they have made changes to the lists of deposits and withdrawals, or perhaps they have begun to think differently about how they spend their energy.

### Introducing accounts and colour coding
In this session, we want to introduce the idea that there are different 'kinds of energy', or different Energy Bank accounts. We want to introduce the concepts that social withdrawals are also deposits, because they help to protect against loneliness, and that healthy foods, exercise and sunlight may be withdrawals in one sense (e.g. due to sensory sensitivities, dislikes or simply the cost of 'getting started' due to impaired executive functions), but they also build a layer of protection, making the body and nervous system more resilient towards depression, anxiety and stress as well as contributing to improved quality of sleep.

As a metaphor, we could say that different accounts correspond to expenses we normally have in a house budget. The social account may be your utilities bill, which may or may not be due every month, but we do know that if you do not pay your utilities, they will eventually be shut off, making life more difficult. You will be cold with no heating in the house, or hot or humid with no air conditioning, it will be dark at night without electricity, and so on. Life without social activities will likewise become 'dark and cold' in the sense that loneliness is likely to take hold, and on a neurological level, your access to deposits of oxytocin will be restricted.

The physical account may be your insurance, protecting you from the most severe consequences should an accident happen. Granted, there will still be 'expenses' associated with the accident, but not nearly the same as they would be without the insurance. In a very real way, taking care of our physical health contributes to protecting us (to a certain extent) from illness and injury, and makes recovery from these quicker and easier. Furthermore, it contributes to the production of many of the neurotransmitters we need to have a healthy nervous system, as we have explored.

In reality, both of these 'accounts' focus on balancing the neuro-transmitters and hormones that need to be balanced in order to stabilize our stress threshold as much as possible. However, they have different foci and the expenses associated with the social and health account activities can be vastly different and often depend to a great degree on the person's personality and cognitive pro-file. Someone who has greater difficulties reading other people's behaviour and facial expressions or a slower processing time for social information will have a higher 'social account bill', but can be just as vulnerable to loneliness as anyone else.

You will remember from Chapter 7 that these accounts can be colour coded to make planning a day or a week more efficient. In this book, we use red for the social account, and blue for the physical account, but the choice of colour is up to you/your client.

Which other accounts, activity categories and colours would it make sense to use?

Try taking the list of deposits and withdrawals, and talk about which accounts the different activities may belong in, and what colours the client would want to use for each account. Colour coding should help the person get a quick overview of whether there is balance in their day, week or month. Therefore, the colours should be different enough to quickly distinguish, but also need to be colours that the person is comfortable looking at. Take into account sensory and emotional sensitivities to colours when choosing. As previously mentioned, some people prefer stronger colours, whereas others are overwhelmed by these, and respond better to a combination of pastel colours.

Be careful to explain that no activity category is inherently negative. As you may recall from the chapter on colour coding, a category such as 'draining' refers to the relative size of the costs, rather than whether the activities are enjoyable or not.

### Follow-up on deposits and withdrawals lists
Check if there may be additions that the client has thought of since last time. Remember, this is not homework, and it is important that the client does not get the sense that they should feel guilty about not having made additions since the last session. However, if they or a family member or friend have thought of anything new, it should be added. The conversation around different accounts may also spark ideas. Throughout Energy Accounting there will be the recognition of new sources of energy depletion or infusion.

### Making one change based on the conversations so far
In this session, discuss briefly the question: Are there rules or guidelines that relate to the accounts/colours? For example, should each day have a few hours of 'green'/restoring time at the beginning or end of the day?

Should there be no more than one big or 'draining' activity per day, such as school, a party or larger get-together, or should there be a maximum or minimum number of social activities per week?

It is important that the strictness of such a rule or guideline is discussed as some may understand it very literally at a time when they may not have to be so literal. When we use the word 'rule' here, it is meant in the sense that it is a general rule which can be bent or an exception to the rule identified. For example, if there is a rule that says 'There should be one mental health day per week', and one week the person is invited to participate in something every day (or both weekend days after a week full of school or work), they may choose to try out not having their mental health day that week and perhaps making notes of any consequences for their energy levels. It may then be appropriate to consider when the next available date is that they can have a mental health day, or whether their evenings may be allotted to mental health or self-care activities to a higher degree for the following week. If a client perceives the word 'rule' as being very strict and concrete, it may be better to frame them as guidelines rather than rules.

## STAGE 3: PSYCHOEDUCATION ON STRESS
Stage 3 focuses on:

- evaluation
- psychoeducation on stress
- relating the knowledge on stress to the person's experience
- giving hope and encouragement for change.

### Evaluation
Once again, we begin each session by asking the client how the content and discussion of the last session may have had an impact.

We may use the following partial sheet as an inspiration – the full sheet will be introduced later.

*Evaluation*

| Question | Answer, issues to be discussed, current strategies | Suggested strategies |
|---|---|---|
| Are there value estimates from the deposits and withdrawals discussion that need to be corrected? Perhaps there are days or weeks that should be balanced, but do not seem to be in reality. | | |
| Which points or topics from former sessions have been most beneficial to accessing new strategies or perspectives? | | |
| Are there any key deposits or withdrawals since the last session that should be discussed? | | |

## Psychoeducation on stress

When we educate people on stress, it is a combination of explaining how the brain and nervous system work, how the body responds, and applying the information to their personal experiences. It is important to check in during the session to see whether they understand, and whether they can recognize the signs of stress in themselves or if they find the knowledge useful. It can be helpful to employ metaphors suggested by the person to make it easier to remember, not just for the client but also for the clinician.

You may include the following points:

- *How do stress responses happen?* This is a quick introduction to what happens in the brain, within the limbic system. We find it useful to include the amygdala, hippocampus, hypothalamus and pituitary gland in the explanation, so as to provide education which can help to quantify the physiology and attach a metaphorical story to the explanation. It can also be useful, especially with those who have sensory processing differences, to talk about the thalamus and its role in filtering sensory information before it reaches the amygdala. Note here that input to the olfactory sense goes directly to the amygdala.

    Maja has found it beneficial to explain in this general format: the thalamus acts as a kind of sensory sieve, which can be more or less effective. The information then goes to the amygdala, the big red panic button of the brain, which tends to think that lots of things are scary and dangerous. Luckily, the hippocampus is there to chat with the amygdala. The hippocampus can be called the librarian of the brain – that is, it is not necessarily where memories are stored, but is responsible for finding the relevant information. The hippocampus and amygdala discuss whether or not an event is scary or dangerous – for example, a sound in the woods or a person approaching you – and come to an agreement. That information is then passed on to the hypothalamus, the thermometer of the body. The hypothalamus recognizes that to deal with the situation, your brain and body are going to need stress hormones in order to react and adapt. The hypothalamus sends this message to the pituitary gland which secretes cortisol and adrenaline.

The explanation can be very quick and informative, but can also be accompanied by pictures, or spending more time making it entertaining and fun, depending on the client. Perhaps the client wants to help figure out what situation is causing a stress response, and thus help to 'tell the story', so to speak. The more you can engage the client in a metaphor or story that makes sense to them, the more likely they are to be able to recall this information, if they need to.

- *What starts a stress response?* The four listed by research are novelty, unpredictability, a decreased sense of control, and a threat to one's ego. Remember here that one's own thoughts can also be a threat to ego. Thoughts such as 'I am not good enough' can create or enhance stress responses.

  Again, it is important to make this personal and relatable to the client. Discuss with them in which situations they might be able to recognize these stress response causes. Which thoughts do they have which might be threats to their ego? When do they feel a lack of control? How does unpredictability or new experiences make them feel? Be as concrete as possible. If the client likes this way of exploring, you can spend more time on this, or return to the topic during a later session.

- *What mediates stress responses?* Here we explain that inter-pretation/cognitive evaluation of the stressor can increase or decrease the strength of the stress response, and that a balanced nervous system is generally more resilient to stressors, as well as better able to end the stress response when appropriate. Once again, investigate with the client how they might be able to recognize this in their own lives. They are likely to have tried something that felt a bit daunt-ing the first time they did it, but which they have got better at, and now feel neutral or even positive towards. This could be solving a problem in a game, travelling by themselves (even over short distances), or talking to a specific person.

- *Bigger/more extreme stress responses make it more difficult to think rationally, use strategies or learn that you can handle the stressor.* An example here is that in exposure to a phobia, if we were to begin by confronting a person directly with an extreme form of their phobia, their brain would not be able to learn that situations involving their phobia were actually okay and manageable. An example of this could be a person with arachnophobia (fear of spiders) being asked to hold a live tarantula in their hands during the first session. This would not work and would be more likely to induce a panic attack. Instead, we seek to have the stress responses be mild enough that the therapeutic strategies can be used and the person has enough access to rational thinking ability that they can learn to cope with the situation. The person with arachnophobia might be able to begin with talking about spiders, or looking at a picture of a cartoon spider.

  As in exposure therapy approaches, we recommend creating a 'ladder' or hierarchy of stress-inducing situations and making a plan for the lowest rung on the ladder. Always be mindful to adjust whenever necessary, and to err on the side of caution. Using this approach in stress management should be a carefully monitored process, and should not begin until you and your client have done plenty of investigation as to the reasons why certain situations or activities are stressful. As noted earlier in the book, please keep in mind that exposure therapy does not work to reduce the impact of sensory sensitivities.

- *Stress hormones and what they do.* The stress hormones are adrenaline and cortisol. Explain what their functions are in a healthy nervous system. For some people, it can be highly relevant to talk about cortisol causing damage to the nervous system, including several parts of the brain;

however, remember to explain that the brain can heal itself. Long-term stress inhibits healing and so can slow the process of improvement, but the brain and nervous system can recover from stress. Research has shown that following neuronal branch deterioration during stress, anxiety and depression, once treated, neuronal branching does recover (Gerlach 2008).

- *The sympathetic and parasympathetic nervous system.* We encourage having visuals to go along with the explanation. Remember also that the idea is not to say that activating either nervous system is bad, but that a balance is important. Both are necessary, but over-activation of the nervous systems can cause a lot of discomfort mentally and physically.

- *Which neurotransmitters and hormones can we work on balancing?* We find it useful to focus on these five: serotonin, oxytocin, dopamine, endorphins and acetylcholine. The first two are involved in feedback inhibition and, as such, ending the stress response when appropriate. Dopamine can be explained as 'the good adrenaline', but it is also involved in our motivation to do anything at all. For those who may be using Energy Accounting where, for example, depression or attention disorders are involved, the person's sensitivity to dopamine may be a theme in later sessions. Endorphins are central in having access to feeling good and relaxed. Acetylcholine enables neurons to communicate with one another, and is linked to many functions, one being learning ability. See EnergyAccounting.com for more information regarding these neurotransmitters.

In this psychoeducation topic, be mindful of varying the amount of detail depending on the client. Some will find it interesting and exciting, while others will be waiting for it to become relevant to practical behaviour in everyday life. One of the characteristics of autism is an interest in seeking knowledge on a topic of personal interest or value, and some clients may even come back and give you a lecture on details which you left out. An activity that you may consider is to ask the client to conduct research on the internet for relevant information, articles and graphics which you can review and discuss during subsequent sessions.

### Relating the knowledge on stress to the person's experience

It is important to spend some time figuring out what the client can use this knowledge for in their daily lives. For some, the mere knowledge and understanding that what is happening to them at certain points in time is 'just' a stress response can be helpful. There can be a distancing from the event in a sense. 'It's not who I am, my brain is just trying to cope with this situation. If I wait, my brain will calm down.'

A key aspect is to figure out what their acute and long-term stress symptoms are. For this, use the list of stress symptoms as a starting point. Even if they are not certain which apply or not, the list can serve as a way to begin talking about what is normal for them, what may be a long-term symptom they are already experiencing, or at what times of day and in which situations they can remember experiencing the symptom. For such a discussion, it may likewise be useful to have the 'symptoms' of activation of the parasympathetic and sympathetic nervous system at hand. This may also spark conversation and insight.

Eventually, you want to increase interoception, insight and self-understanding such that the person is more able to notice acute symptoms which may be leading to an anxiety attack, meltdown or even a needless argument with a loved one, and they can instead take precautions, communicate with their surroundings and take care of themselves. Likewise, with long-term stress, being able to see stress or a depression forming and 'nipping it in the bud' by making changes to their daily lives is highly preferable.

If the person is okay with the concept of therapeutic 'homework' and can see a point in it, there can be homework assigned for next time. There may be an aversion to the term 'homework' which is associated with unpleasant memories of school days. An alternative term is a project or assignment. It may be to write down any more symptoms they can think of, or it could be to notice and write down an example of when they felt stressed, what symptoms they experience, and what happened before and after this.

## Giving hope and encouragement for change

Importantly, before the session or stage is over, the client should have learned a fast-acting stress-management strategy such as a breathing exercise, distracting themselves with something, or a progressive muscle relaxation technique. For the clinician, it will be useful to have a range of options available, and you may find that it is helpful to have a list, possibly illustrated, for the client to look over.

Go through one or two concrete exercises and have them try these during the session. Be realistic about the effects and reiterate that practice makes perfect. This is why we do not recommend learning a whole handful of strategies all at once. Rather, learning one or two makes it easier to remember your options and therefore easier to try to implement them in daily life.

It is okay if they forget to use the strategy at first. This is normal. It takes time for a strategy to become cognitively available during times you need it. For this reason, it may be easiest for the person to begin implementing the strategy during situations where they feel only a very little stressed, a 'low rung on the ladder'. It is in these situations they have better access to their thinking abilities, their memory included. Indeed, they may receive better effects if they begin by practising the strategy during calm moments. This way, the brain learns the strategy while learning capacity is higher, and the strategy may then be more easily implemented when needed.

They may not feel the effect of it helping right away. This can be due to impaired interoception or disrupted feedback inhibition, or it can be because they are still new to the exercise and it still feels awkward, weird or they overthink it. It may also be that this particular exercise is not for them, but it will take up to four months before you can really tell if a strategy is helping. The key, therefore, is patience and practice.

## STAGE 4: MONITORING WELL-BEING
Stage 4 focuses on:

- evaluation
- what is well-being?
- how can we 'diagnose' well-being?
- what are your symptoms of well-being?
- monitoring well-being structure
- plans for action.

### Evaluation
Once again, we begin each appointment by asking the client how the content and discussion of the last session may have had an impact.

We may use the following partial sheet as an inspiration – the full sheet will be introduced later.

*Evaluation*

| Question | Answer, issues to be discussed, current strategies | Suggested strategies |
|---|---|---|
| Are there value estimates from the deposits and withdrawals discussion that need to be corrected? Perhaps there are days or weeks that should be balanced, but do not seem to be in reality. | | |
| Which points or topics from former sessions have been most beneficial to accessing new strategies or perspectives? | | |
| Are there any key deposits or withdrawals since the last session that should be discussed? | | |

## What is well-being?

As we discussed in the chapter on well-being, the state of well-being is highly subjective and individual. Just as with stress, it will be different situations and activities that cause a person to feel well. For this reason, this session begins by examining what well-being means for this particular person.

Some people, when they hear the word 'well-being', think of images or descriptions of people who are happy. Perhaps they are meditating, being in nature, having a drink with friends, smiling, laughing. Perhaps the images are inspired by social media and advertising portrayals of happiness from buying a specific product, or perhaps they are the result of perceived expectations – how they believe others expect them to live. This version of well-being – as we touched on in the well-being chapter – seems always very far away. A person who thinks of well-being in this way will likely perceive themselves as unhappy, as having not achieved what others have, even as a failure. If this is relevant, the first part of the session, and in some cases an entire session, is devoted to discussing the question, 'What is well-being really?'

It is important that the person comes to their own conclusions. If someone else merely tells them how the world works, the answer will not be integrated, meaning it will be something they have heard rather than something they have realized and come to understand and believe. This means we may provide perspectives and ask questions to help the person come to their own conclusion. For example, do they believe that a person in such an image feels that way all the time?

It may be useful to use knowledge from the last session – psychoeducation on stress – as a jumping-off point. Here we talked about neurotransmitters and hormones, and their effects. When people are smiling, laughing and feeling 'happiness', what neurotransmitters are in play? Are some of them perhaps very dominant during such an emotion? All emotions are passing, or are supposed to be. If you feel sad all the time, or apathetic, we might call this depression. If you feel worried all the time, we might call this generalized anxiety – though there are different forms of anxiety, of course. Would it make sense that others feel happy all the time or would this also be a 'diagnosis'?

Well-being, in terms of quality of life, is more a matter of overall contentment rather than happiness or glee. Well-being is not euphoria or bliss. It is more neutral.

Well-being means having balance in your neurotransmitters, it means having energy to do things in your life – but remember that everyone's optimal energy capacity will be different. It also means having an accurate and positive-leaning self-perception. For many, it also means having enough time on a daily basis where they do not feel they have to mask or camouflage their authentic self.

What this means, of course, is that well-being goes far beyond stress management. However, they go hand in hand, and there is no reason to not aim for a general improvement in the person's life.

## How can we 'diagnose' well-being?

For some people, it can be hard to know if you are feeling better or worse before the change is very significant. People sometimes think back to a time in their lives when they were happier or felt worse and are able to recognize that change, but changes that happen over a month or a few months can be more difficult to pinpoint. Furthermore, people who have difficulties with interoception often have to rely on behavioural cues to tell them how they are feeling. As an autistic adult said, 'I only know what I am feeling by seeing what I am doing.'

It is important that we use this stage to reiterate that it is okay and normal to have a difficult time knowing what well-being is and how it feels. As a society, we often talk about stress, anxiety or depression – still in somewhat vague terms but we do talk about it – and so people sometimes have more references to talk about these things. But many people do not have the language to really talk about the thoughts and feelings associated with well-being or recognize it in themselves, and while this is unfortunate, it is okay. That is why we talk about it in these sessions and explore the concept of well-being.

Any diagnostic criteria are based around a norm. What is the norm, what falls outside and what are the patterns in behaviour and symptoms we can recognize and form criteria around? Not everyone has every symptom, but symptoms, and patterns in symptoms, can point us in the direction of saying 'this person may have depression', for example. In the same way, it can be useful to talk about symptoms of well-being. How can we diagnose well-being in people?

It is important to recognize that the signs of well-being may be more visible to those around a person than to themselves. For this reason, family and friends can often be included in this process to great benefit.

A part of discovering how to manage stress and enhance quality of life and well-being is being able to spot when you feel good. Because emotions can be fleeting experiences, happiness is often something that lasts seconds or minutes rather than hours and days, while contentment is the more neutral, lasting state. This means that there will be symptoms that are short term and long term.

Earlier in the book, we divided stressors into situational factors and more long-term basic conditions and primary factors. We do this because we can see the effect of stressors over shorter or longer periods of time. In the same way, well-being symptoms can be situational – fleeting or longer term. We may call long-term symptoms primary, perhaps. If this word does not appeal to you or your client, use a different one. It is not the name of the category that matters, but the concept.

As with symptoms of stress, a person will likely also have internal, emotional and psychological symptoms of well-being, as well as external, behavioural symptoms.

So now that we know how to diagnose well-being, we need to find the symptoms that apply to the individual.

## What are your symptoms of well-being?

Figuring out a person's symptoms of well-being can be much more difficult than figuring out stress symptoms, but the process is, in many ways, the same. We begin with a discussion. For this discussion, we encourage you to use the now personalized list of stress symptoms and the general list of well-being symptoms for inspiration. The personalized stress symptoms can be used as inspiration in that they may include behavioural signs that are absent when the person feels well, or where they maybe do the opposite when feeling well. For example, when stressed, the person may withdraw from their usual online social activity. When feeling well, they may be very active and engaging socially (this may still be online) and may sometimes initiate social interaction.

In this way, use what you have already found out as a starting point. When feeling well, certain things may still not be great, or easy, but perhaps they stop being a *problem* that drains the person of energy. An example of this may be someone who has a mild sensory sensitivity with tooth-brushing or showering. If they are stressed, this is often one of the things they unconsciously stop doing or postpone, whereas during times of well-being it is slightly more automatic or easier to get through, although the sensory sensitivity is still there. It is more manageable.

Another way to discuss symptoms of well-being, especially situational symptoms, is to talk about when the person feels happy, when they smile, when they feel relaxed. What are the situations when these things happen, such as engaging in a passionate interest, being in nature or with someone who is an enjoyable companion? Delve into details regarding these situations. If the person has a hard time remembering when they last felt relaxed or smiled, they may instead remember a situation when they felt less stressed than usual, or when they did not feel quite as sad – look for situations where they felt closer to neutral than sad. What is the pattern of those situations and what is significant about them?

This can be important both for finding behavioural symptoms they had not considered, as well as providing some ideas for the plans for action.

Write down some symptoms of well-being. The list may well expand over time, and especially with input from close friends or family.

| | Internal | External |
|---|---|---|
| Situational | | |
| Primary/ Long-term | | |

## Monitoring well-being structure

Now that we know the individual symptoms of stress and well-being, we can set up ways to monitor well-being. Use the monitoring well-being chapter as inspiration.

Importantly, not every type of monitoring should be used. We use the 80/20 principle. If we can spend less energy implementing one new strategy that provides most of what we need, there is no point implementing three or four strategies because this will carry a much greater energy cost as well. Here are some points to note:

- *Have a close friend or family member watch out for changes.* With the client's consent, share the programme with trusted family members and friends and let them know that they can help you and the effectiveness of the programme by sharing with you any signs and situations they have noticed that change your client's well-being.

- *Ask the client to rate how they feel at the start and end of the day*. Create a numerical scale of well-being that ranges from 1 to 100 or from 1 to 10, for example. For the scale of 1–100, for example, the client's natural or neutral state of well-being could be rated as 50, with numbers below 50 indicating a decreasing sense of well-being and above 50 indicating a greater sense of well-being. The client makes a note of the numerical value of well-being at the start and end of the day and perhaps at specific times during the day. You could also use scales for depression symptoms, perceived energy or other factors you would like to track.

- *See changes in routine/lack of energy as a warning sign*. When we keep track of our routines or perceived energy, we may notice that certain changes are warning signs of decreasing well-being. Very often, changes in diet or hygiene routines and motivation can be signs of acutely low stress capacity, and if these changes persist they can be a warning of increased stress, anxiety or depression.

## Plans for action

Having a plan for what to do if well-being is decreasing is important, as well as making that plan or those plans concrete and sharing them with trusted people who can help to make sure they are acted on.

Here are some ideas for plans. Some of them are ideal for future sessions or for discussion with a close friend or family member who can help, others are actions the person themselves can take. Keep in mind these are just ideas and there may be many alternatives that are not included here.

These plans for action will also be central in future sessions or stages as the ability to work with them independently will be a great tool for the person going forward.

### Evaluation or investigation

The first questions to ask are why and how is well-being decreasing? Is there increased stress, sadness, agitation or other emotional changes? Did something happen to trigger this? Is there an immediate answer or perhaps something hidden over the last week or two? If not, go further back. Are there primary stress factors that have been building over time?

It is important that the client develops a sense of trust with the clinician, as some factors such as trauma in childhood and recent flashbacks may take some time to be disclosed and incorporated in Energy Accounting. However, when a client is able to do monitoring and evaluations with a trusted individual, or more independently, the inclusion of such sensitive information may happen more readily.

Here we may begin with any guidelines that are already implemented – have they been followed, did they not work, do they need to change? For example, instead of one mental health day per week, perhaps right now the person needs two? Or perhaps there is something preventing the guideline from being followed right now?

It can be beneficial to use a standard model for evaluation and investigation, such as those included in this book or on the EnergyAccounting.com handouts.

### Let someone know/Ask for help

There may be one or several people the person trusts enough to contact if they discover they are not feeling emotionally well or are energy depleted. This may include a professional support person or clinician, but can also be a family member or close friend.

Sometimes, people can find out they are not okay and need help or some positive changes, but without knowing what it is that is wrong or what changes they may need. This is why seeking out another person's perspective can be so helpful. They can help to look at possible causes for the decline in well-being, as well as possible solutions.

If the decline in well-being is acute rather than long-term, the solutions can be quite simple but may still require, or be easier with, another person helping.

People who are very social by nature may instinctively seek others out for help, or be more prone to do so, even if it is difficult in the moment. People who are more introverted, have a smaller social network or have a degree of social anxiety may need to know exactly who to contact, in which way, and during what timeframe they can expect a reply. The person who is providing support may also need instruction in how to best help in these situations, not only for their benefit, but also so that the person seeking help knows what to expect.

### Use a strategy that aligns with the problem

As clinicians and support staff, we must have a wide variety of strategies available to us at all times, to help each person we work with to find the strategies that best suit them. However, it is important to not overwhelm people with options. For that reason, we recommend starting with two strategies – one fast-acting to cope with acute stress, and one longer-term strategy, to cope with baseline well-being being impacted. Once these have been practised and incorporated, or you have reason to think they will not work for the person, try something new. It is important to recognize that every strategy does not work for every person, and that this is okay.

Often, the fast-acting strategies we begin with are things like a breathing exercise or using distraction. These can help curb a meltdown before it happens, but do not do anything about the cause. For that reason, they rarely stand alone. However, they are still useful.

Longer term, it may be necessary to figure out if there could be activities that could help the person's neurotransmitters to become more balanced. You can start by using our pre-written lists of activities that are connected to neurotransmitters, available in the downloadable material but eventually you can discuss which other activities may belong on each list for this person.

Lastly, of course, a strategy may be to make changes to the daily or weekly routine. Use the Energy Accounting bank tool to explore when and how the accounts are being overdrawn and find a way to make changes that will balance the budget.

Once your client is able to use their strategies independently, you can more readily add more options, building up their toolbox, so that they themselves are able to choose which strategy to use in any given situation. The end goal will be that we as clinicians are not needed in our client's life, as they have become so knowledgeable about their own Energy Accounting that they act independently or with a support person who is available to them at all times.

## STAGE 5: NEW STRATEGIES
Stage 5 focuses on:

- evaluation
- learning new strategies
- finding more ways to strengthen deposits and lessen cost of withdrawals.

### Evaluation
From now on, we want to include regular evaluations, taking into account the 80/20 rule.

20 per cent of the effort put in by the person to implement changes should ideally result in 80 per cent of the results. It is, therefore, the strategies that only take that 20 per cent effort that we are attempting to identify and hold on to.

Begin by talking about what you have done so far. What has worked, what has not, what have been the barriers to the programme, what has made an impact in the person's way of thinking, what has not?

Are there any strategies the person feels they would very much like to be better at implementing, but there seems to be a barrier to them achieving this? Very often, executive impairments, attention disorders, depression, anxiety and so on result in it being difficult to actually implement new strategies. The barriers are different, but it is commonly things like lacking energy, forgetting, not seeing the point (in the situation, even though it makes sense when speaking with you), or getting distracted. From here, the hurdle is to find ways around these barriers. It is unlikely that simply talking about it will make a difference, and if the person could break the barriers themselves, they would have. This is why they need you to help come up with ideas. Are there external prompts that could work? Are there sentences they can tell themselves to find energy, well-being, meaning or hope? Is there anyone in their support system who can help to follow up or provide reminders in a good way?

Lastly, we want to see if there are any patterns that may be emerging from using Energy Accounting. Perhaps in the daily tracking, or in using colour coding, some pattern can be seen. Are there symptoms of stress/well-being that change on specific days, times of day or under specific circumstances? Are there days that should – according to the numbers from the Energy Bank discussions – be fine, but which turn out not to be? This may show itself through unexpected meltdowns, increased tiredness the day after, social withdrawal or a general increase in stress symptoms that may be building. What we would be hoping to achieve is the opposite, of course. A general decrease in stress symptoms, fewer meltdowns, a decrease in exhaustion and more positive connection and engagement.

Note that any results from making changes generally take up to four months to fully show, and as we are dealing with people's lives, we are never able to plan everything. Changes will happen that we cannot foresee, which will affect the energy budget. However, we want to try to identify when these changes happen, and catch information we might have previously overlooked, over time.

While everything should always be personalized to the client, including the evaluations, these questions and points will provide a general idea of what it would be useful to include. You can use the following questionnaire as an inspiration or guide. Only fill out the questions that are relevant, and skip any that do not make sense to discuss.

*Evaluation*

| Question | Answer, issues to be discussed, current strategies | Suggested strategies |
|---|---|---|
| Are there value estimates from the deposits and withdrawals discussion that need to be corrected? Perhaps there are days or weeks that should be balanced, but do not seem to be in reality. | | |

| Question | Answer, issues to be discussed, current strategies | Suggested strategies |
|---|---|---|
| Are there any points to be made from monitoring systems that have been put in place? (For example, changes in stress/well-being symptoms, tracking notes.) | | |
| Are there any notable patterns emerging from daily tracking, colour coding or other sources of information?<br><br>Look for stress or well-being symptoms that occur on specific days, times of day or in specific circumstances. | | |
| Are there any strategies that seem to be working badly, are hard to execute/implement? | | |

| Question | Answer, issues to be discussed, current strategies | Suggested strategies |
|---|---|---|
| Which strategies seem, at the moment, to be providing the best pay-off? | | |
| Which points or topics from former sessions have been most beneficial to accessing new strategies or perspectives? | | |
| Are there any key deposits or withdrawals since the last session that should be discussed? | | |

For this type of evaluation, it may be useful to include any notes which the support system may have, and they may indeed send their thoughts regularly to you either through the client or, if the client agrees, directly to you. It is, naturally, of utmost importance that the client feels respected, in control of their own programme and informed at all times. At the very beginning of Stage 1, there should be discussion regarding confidentiality.

The evaluation sheet is available at EnergyAccounting.com/handouts.

### Learning new strategies

When managing stress and seeking to improve quality of life, it is useful to build up a repertoire of strategies, such that a number of strategies are available at any given time. We can think of it as 'adding tools to our Energy Accounting toolbox or library'.

Common strategies to add include breathing exercises, mindfulness meditation (often guided, and adjusted to autistic people's needs), using art or journalling as a form of expression, yoga or walking, or using realistic thoughts as an answer to negative ruminating thoughts.

Other strategies that may be useful, specifically for those who deal with anxiety attacks, rumination or sensory overload, are the use of fidget toys, sensory toys or music as a distraction.

Try to add only one new strategy at a time. As previously mentioned, for the person learning a new strategy, having several added in one go can be overwhelming, which means that often it is useful to quickly present a few options and then together figure out which one to learn today. Factors in choosing include how much the person believes that the strategy will work, and how difficult it is to implement.

Go through the strategy together. For example, go through a mindfulness meditation together – begin with only five minutes. Find a guided meditation that the person feels good about doing (take into account their preferences for any background music, bells, the language/word choices in the meditation). For clinicians, it is useful to again have a small repertoire available to use. Autistic people will tend to prefer more concrete language and fewer abstract metaphors, and may even like to have a countdown on a screen if they are unable to keep their eyes closed throughout – it can help them to get to know the meditation and know what to expect while they are learning to use mindfulness meditation.

While the majority of autistic adolescents and adults benefit from mindfulness meditation, we have found that about a third have genuine difficulty meditating and may describe the experience as confusing or aversive.

Importantly, the person should know that it is okay in the next session to let you know if they absolutely cannot use the new strategy and they need a different one. This may mean the strategy simply is not for them, or that it currently is too high a barrier of entry. This is perfectly normal and is a part of finding out what works for them. Discovering that a strategy is not great for them right now does not mean that time was wasted; rather, it means that we have gathered more information.

### Finding more ways to strengthen deposits and lessen cost of withdrawals

Lastly, if there is time, go back to the initial Energy Bank discussion. Are there strategies that could be implemented to strengthen deposits and lessen the cost of withdrawals – making the budget more efficient – that have not already been attempted?

This could involve using noise-cancelling headphones, sensory toys or fidget toys in certain situations or circumstances, such as during breaktimes at school, while studying, at the dinner table or while on the train or bus. When it comes to transportation, it may also be useful to consider reducing the time spent, or the mode of transportation, or the number of bus or train changes.

When we go through daily or common activities in this way, the mindset is to find small, practical ways to improve daily life and prioritize better how the person's energy is spent.

## STAGE 6: INTERACTING ENERGY ACCOUNTS
Stage 6 focuses on:

- evaluation
- considering interacting energy accounts.

### *Evaluation*
We begin with evaluation, and you can use the evaluation sheet as an inspiration or guide. Only fill out the questions that are relevant, and skip any that do not make sense to discuss.

The evaluation sheet is available at EnergyAccounting.com/handouts.

### *Considering interacting energy accounts*
In this session, we begin exploring how people's energy accounts affect each other. This is primarily useful for those who live with others, either as a family or collective, or it could be some form of protected living or a work or school setting.

Often, there are points in the initial discussion which can be helpful in starting this conversation. For example, many people, especially autistic people, are influenced by the mood of those around them. We call this emotional empathy, and the experience is often that someone's negative mood can be 'infectious' and energy draining. If someone they live with or work with is having a bad day, and they are in a bad mood, this creates a withdrawal from both people's accounts. Many people have, during the discussion, some version of social activity where the other person's mood, personality, behaviour or general situation is a factor in the energy cost of the activity. This is a good point to begin a conversation about interacting energy accounts.

For the first session regarding this subject, the main focus is to become conscious of interacting energy accounts. The framework and metaphor of Energy Accounting is used to introduce a way of thinking about how the person is affected by others and how they affect others. It is very important, especially for those who may be sensitive to feelings such as guilt and shame, that this topic does not become a way to underscore, for example, how badly a person's meltdown affects their family members. Rather, the topic should be used to encourage empathy and understanding towards one another, and to explore how each person might contribute positively to others' energy accounts. It is, however, very likely that negative examples do come up, and in these moments we encourage the clinician to discuss in a non-judgemental way how everyone experiences moments when they are not acting based on what is best and rational, but from an emotional state. One way to look at it is to say that the frontal lobes – which allow us to control and monitor our own behaviour and its consequences – have been temporarily switched off. The person is now controlled by their amygdala, or their limbic system. Another example of not being fully in control is when we act on 'autopilot', forgetting to consider the consequences of our actions.

A good way to move forward is to discuss what strategies or agreements can be made in the household regarding what to do in certain situations, in order to affect each other's energy accounts in a better way.

Depending on personality, interoception, introspective abilities, degree of emotional empathy and much more, this topic is more useful to some than others, and so again we must emphasize the importance of personalizing the programme to suit each individual. If you are working with someone for whom this makes no sense at all, then the idea has been planted but no more time should be spent on the topic now.

You can spend as much or as little time on this topic as you and the client deem suitable, but we do generally find that introducing the concept will end up paying off for the client, even if this pay-off happens years after the fact.

Sub-topics here could include the following:

- Which people are energy-depleting 'black holes' and which are restorative/energy suns? Begin by focusing on immediate family, friends, support staff and colleagues – anyone the person interacts with on a regular basis. If family members are present for the session, it may be best to not focus on them, as this can sometimes create tense situations for everyone involved.

- What are the resulting changes in each person's energy budget when one person has a bad day, bad mood, meltdown? How much energy does it take for the child, how much for the parents, and why? What strategies or agreements can be implemented to alleviate this? Likewise, what changes occur when someone has the energy to do something good for a family member? Does this function as a deposit for the other person?

- What social strategies can be used to repair relationships after conflicts, criticism or negative interpersonal experiences – that is, strategies that lower the cost of the conflict for one or several energy accounts?

This topic can develop into sessions that focus on social understanding, both in terms of communication and interaction, but also the interoceptive aspects, and strategies that may help to make things easier in the longer run. Metaphors can help to reduce the amount of energy depletion; for example, when someone is radiating negative energy, imagine holding up a shield or wearing armour, or that the negative energy is rain and you are opening an umbrella to stay dry. Again, this will not work for everyone, but some do find it very helpful.

## STAGE 7: ADJUSTMENTS TO SUDDEN AND SYSTEMATIC CHANGES

Stage 7 focuses on:

- evaluation
- adjusting to systematic changes
- adjusting to sudden changes.

### Evaluation

We begin with evaluation, and you can use the evaluation sheet as an inspiration or guide. Only fill out the questions that are relevant, and skip any that do not make sense to discuss.

The evaluation sheet is available at EnergyAccounting.com/handouts.

### Adjusting to systematic changes

Adjusting to changes in life is something that people often do in one form or another, but in many cases, they do not think about what and how they do it. For autistic people, changes can disrupt their entire rhythm and result in meltdowns.

The purpose of going through systematic changes with a client is to make a conscious process and choice out of what can otherwise feel like chaos. We want, instead, for the adjustments to become a strategy that is employed purposefully by the person and thereby empowers them.

Begin by discussing again which changes can be identified that are systematic or anticipated. On a weekly basis, this might be things we do not consider as 'changes' but part of the rhythm of things; for example, a scheduled personal or public holiday, or at the weekend, a child or adolescent switching between staying with one parent and the other.

On a yearly basis, common examples include, as mentioned earlier in the book, holidays, the pollen season, seasonal or winter depression, or it could be something related to their interest, such as going to the same convention every year.

Once you have a list of systematic or anticipated changes that apply to the client, choose an item on the list which you will be working with. Perhaps the client has a preference, one that is particularly difficult to deal with, or one where they have more hope that coping with it differently will be possible.

Talk about this item in more depth. What about the change is difficult, and what might be possible to adjust?

## Anticipated Change and Sudden Change

In this resource, we look at how anticipated change and sudden change may have different impacts on stress and energy levels, and how they can be accommodated to minimize their impact.

One client told Maja that Christmas and New Year were particularly difficult. They had two families to celebrate with, one of which was very active during the holidays. This meant that instead of a one-day Christmas celebration, this person, although they were adult, felt they had no choice but to participate in four days full of social activity, sometimes with close to 20 people. Then, there were only a few days to relax before New Year's Eve, which meant more socializing, with added sensory difficulties due not only to fireworks, but also to exhaustion, which meant their 'sensory filter' felt as if it was missing. They managed to get through this, but with many meltdowns during the holiday period as a result.

We cannot remove Christmas and New Year from the calendar, nor did the client feel that changes could be made to the general expectation to participate. However, we could perhaps negotiate with the family to not expect the person to participate in just one of the days. We also talked through communicating with the family about having a quiet space to withdraw to, such that they were able to take breaks from the social activity over several of the days. Where this was not possible, we added strategies of how and when to excuse oneself for the night. Furthermore, the days between

Christmas and New Year were allocated as mental health days, which served to remove guilt the person was feeling over how long it took for them to recover. Christmas and New Year are still hard for this person, but they now have a compromise between what they wish they could do and what is realistic for them, in their particular life circumstances.

In this way, adjusting to systematic or anticipated changes is all about finding ways to make the change less negatively impactful to the person's energy levels and mental health. It is important to understand that any adjustments made may not fully solve the problem or entirely alleviate the impact, but should seek to improve the situation and help the person recover as quickly as is possible for them.

## Adjusting to sudden changes

Life often does not go according to plan. As you start the day there is an anticipated sequence of events and expectations. There may be unanticipated changes that require the creation of a plan 'B'. A child or adolescent's usual teacher may not be at school, and so there is a substitute teacher. At work, there may be job changes such as a temporary change in line manager due to illness, new job specifications and priorities, the train may be late, or there may be traffic delays.

Whichever situation might be relevant for the client to discuss – and these situations may well arise between sessions – there are a few different plans for action that can be explored.

One is prioritizing in the Energy Bank – in essence, which activities can be dropped if necessary? For example, a person may have their week planned, when suddenly they are invited to an important social event – perhaps it was not scheduled in good time, or perhaps others forgot to inform them of it. Now, they must quickly figure out how to balance the budget for that week.

The Energy Accounting system will need to be adjusted by engaging in more energy-creating activities and reducing those activities that add to the energy depletion, to reduce the likelihood of a meltdown due to unanticipated changes.

For changes that are so sudden there may not be time to sit down to discuss with a professional, a friend or a family member, it is often beneficial to have a list of close and trusted individuals who can provide support. It may be that not everyone can pick up their phone or answer text messages right away, but if there are several people to reach out to, the chances that someone is available are certainly increased. Discuss with the client: who would be able to provide quick advice in a given situation? Who may best be able to soothe them?

One client came to a session and explained that they had had a very busy and stressful day, and suddenly a train was cancelled when they needed to get somewhere on time. Due to already feeling pressure from the number of tasks that day, this cancellation made their anxiety peak, and they did not know what to do. They ended up calling their mother, who was able to quickly look up a few options for alternative transportation. The two discussed which option would be best, settled on a solution as well as a quick script for them to apologize for being late, and hung up. Although the client ended up being slightly late, they were able to complete their day without much further anxiety. They had spent the evening with self-care activities to do their best to recover. For this client, being able to call someone and find a solution had been a success, and while they hope to get better at thinking of quick solutions in the future, this strategy worked that day.

## STAGE 8: ENHANCING WELL-BEING
Stage 8 focuses on:

- evaluation
- neurotransmitters
- enhancing well-being

## Evaluation
We begin with evaluation, and you can use the evaluation sheet as an inspiration or guide. Only fill out the questions that are relevant, and skip any that do not make sense to discuss.

The evaluation sheet is available at EnergyAccounting.com/ handouts.

## Neurotransmitters
For this stage of the Energy Accounting clinical programme, we want to focus on enhancing well-being. One way to do this is through scheduling activities that contribute to the production and release of neurotransmitters that are beneficial.

This means, if you have not already gone through the five neuro-transmitters during Stage 3, you should do so now. This includes explaining what each neurotransmitter's purpose is, as well as sources of it. You will find the information on promoting resilience in the downloadable material.

It is important to relate each neurotransmitter to real-life activities, and discuss whether the client thinks they have a good balance in neurotransmitters, in a way that feels personal to them. For some people, this way of thinking will never make sense, but for many others, having something to discuss and act on that is more concrete and based on natural and medical science is easier to grasp than abstract discussions about well-being or mental health.

Some clients like to find metaphors to explain each neurotransmitter, while others like to keep the discussion very closely tied to the science – using the correct names, and so on. These clients are also more likely to go home and do their own research on these topics, and they may be more likely to challenge what you have told them. For this reason, it is important that you yourself feel secure in your knowledge when you talk about it. However, it is often equally important to be honest and tell the client that you are not a pro-fessor of neurology, and that you do not necessarily understand all the details of the research. Your job is to understand these things at a practical level – that is, what we can conclude from the research that is applicable to people's day-to-day lives.

For these relatively simple, practical discussions about neurotransmitters, what is presented in this book and in the online resources is often sufficient. You may want to do your own research as well, to have a better personal understanding of the topic.

Importantly, framing well-being in the context of neurotransmitters also provides a way to externalize some of the challenges the client may face. That is, it is not necessarily an inherent part of them to feel the way they do, but rather, there may be a cause to find in the balance of neurotransmitters, and thus, actions to take that can lead to positive change.

For this point, we find that it is generally helpful to take the following approach. Begin with an overall introduction to neurotransmitters – what is a neurotransmitter, which ones will you be going through in the programme and why are they important? Make sure to note that many neurotransmitters overlap or work together in some functions, or interact in other ways. Because of this, there will be some degree of repetition.

Next, discuss one neurotransmitter at a time. Depending on the client, this can take a few minutes, or much more of the session. As you are discussing each neurotransmitter, you may choose to compare the results of the discussion to the client's energy account forms or schedule and see how many activities they have that relate to each transmitter. You could mark which neurotransmitters each activity relates to if you wish (this could be done with symbols such as little stars, dots, an x, or with letters or colours), but this may be too much information to process for you both.

You will also discuss their diet. Because several neurotransmitters depend on both diet and activities in their production and release within our nervous system, this topic should not be avoided. If diet is something that is difficult to discuss due to, for example, sensory processing differences or an eating disorder (either active or not), you can create rules with your client about how to discuss the topic in a way that is manageable for them.

## Enhancing well-being

At this point in the Energy Accounting programme, you and your client will have built up a small toolbox for how to approach enhancing their well-being. Depending on the number of sessions you have at your disposal, you can continue building this toolbox for quite some time, or providing them with ways of doing this independently.

In the neurotransmitter approach, you can discuss which neurotransmitters may be out of balance, and what changes can be made to diet and activities that might help to rebalance the nervous system and promote resilience.

For deposits and withdrawals, including cluster activities, we can find where and how energy is being spent and restored, and changes can be made to rebalance their days.

Colour coding can provide an overview that shows more easily if different types of energy – which often relate to neurotransmitters or stress hormones as well – are not being given enough time, or perhaps given too much time, during a week.

Guidelines for longer-term Energy Accounting may make it easier to plan over weeks and months how the client can balance their energy.

You can also continue adding new strategies as the client feels comfortable with having more options available.

Different forms of monitoring are also available to aid in keeping up Energy Accounting, and preventing or discovering early when stress relapses might occur within and after the programme. These include continuously evaluating and updating Energy Accounting, and the lists of stress and well-being symptoms as these are discovered or change over time.

As time goes on, we should see well-being and quality of life increase, and you may now be at the point where you and your client need to discuss if and how any future contact should be structured.

We recommend that appointments are made available every three to six months for some time, which the client can cancel or move as needed. In between, they can schedule any additional sessions if a crisis should occur.

These much rarer appointments serve the purpose of providing follow-up sessions with a focus on ongoing evaluation and any possible crisis management. People's lives change substantially over time, and they may need someone to discuss with them what to do concerning specific shifts in their lives. Others become highly independent and no longer need these follow-up sessions. In these cases, you can discuss with the client whether they prefer that the appointments are still made, or whether they should contact you if they feel the need to.

In most cases, a one- to two-year period of follow-up sessions every three to six months is recommended. Some people may need more, some far fewer. Again, we encourage that Energy Accounting programmes are tailored to the individual's needs.

● **SEE RESOURCE 14:** *Adaptation of Energy Accounting Method to Different Groups.*

## STRESS AND ENERGY RELAPSE
A stress and energy relapse may occur where a person starts to experience increasing stress and energy depletion despite maintaining Energy Accounting. If this happens, the best strategy for the person is to acknowledge it early, rather than deny that it

is happening. A relapse is not a sign of weakness or failure but may indicate new stress factors or a difficulty achieving energy deposits in their energy account. It is important to recognize any signs of relapse and use these as a reminder to reinvigorate Energy Accounting. The process should begin by monitoring and evaluating. Perhaps the value ranges assigned in their Energy Bank have changed? Perhaps there are new stress factors which have not been included in their Energy Accounting?

There can be anticipated or unexpected events, such as the death of someone close to them or of a pet, a physical illness or an important exam or performance review at work. For some people, the time of year, such as the depth of winter, can increase the level of stress and require greater infusions of energy. It is also recognized that both the lunar and menstrual cycles can have effects on stress and energy, and some people find that they have an ability to cope with life for a defined duration, but regularly, after a specified time, say seven to nine weeks, there is a temporary energy crash. If there is a pattern to relapses, we need to identify this and use the information to adapt Energy Accounting strategies to see if it is possible to either prevent the relapses or at least soften the curve, such that the relapse is not quite so severe.

At the first sign of a stress and energy relapse, we recommend that the individual reviews their Energy Accounting, adding and evaluating any new sources of stress or energy depletion and considering new sources of energy or increasing their engagement in energizing experiences. If it is caught in the early stages, the relapse can be less severe and easier to remedy.

However, if it is not caught early, Energy Accounting can be used to aid in recovery, and the information noted for monitoring and evaluation purposes.

# References

American Psychiatric Association. (2022) *Diagnostic and Statistical Manual of Mental Disorders* (5th ed., text revised). Arlington, VA: APA.

Attwood, A., Evans, C. & Lesko, A. (eds) (2014) *Been There. Done That. Try This! An Aspie's Guide to Life on Earth.* London: Jessica Kingsley Publishers.

Attwood, T. & Garnett, M. (2016) *Exploring Depression, and Beating the Blues.* London: Jessica Kingsley Publishers.

Burke Harris, N. (2018) *The Deepest Well: Healing the Long-Term Effects of Trauma and Adversity.* Boston, MA: Mariner Books.

Cannell, J.J. (2017) Vitamin D and autism, what's new? *Reviews in Endocrine and Metabolic Disorders*, 18, 183–193.

Gotham, K., Unruh, K. & Lord, C. (2015) Depression and its measurement in verbal adolescents and adults with autism spectrum disorder. *Autism*, 19(4), 491–504.

Gerlach, J. (2010). Biologiske årsager til angst. In *Angstbogen: Angstens symptomer, årsager og behandling* (pp. 113–134). PsykiatriFonden.

Health Direct (2023) Dopamine. www.healthdirect.gov.au/dopamine.

Higgins, J., Arnold, S., Weise, J., Pellicano, E. & Trollor, J. (2021) Defining autistic burnout through experts by lived experience: Grounded Delphi method investigating #AutisticBurnout. *Autism*, 25(8), 2356–2369.

Hwang, Y., Arnold, S., Srasuebkul, P. & Trollor, J. (2020) Understanding anxiety in adults on the autism spectrum: An investigation of its relationship with intolerance of uncertainty, sensory sensitivities and repetitive behaviours. *Autism*, 24, 411–422.

*International Classification of Diseases 11* (2022) World Health Organization.

Joshi, G. *et al.* (2013) Psychiatric comorbidity and functioning in a clinically referred population of adults with autism spectrum disorders: A comparative study. *Journal of Autism and Developmental Disorders*, 43, 1314–1325.

Jovevska, S. *et al.* (2020) Sleep quality in autism from adolescence to old age. *Autism in Adulthood*, 2(2), 152–162.

Kelly, A., Garnett, M., Attwood, A. & Peterson, C. (2008) Autism spectrum disorders in children: The impact of family and peer relationships. *Journal of Abnormal Child Psychology*, 36, 1069–1081.

Mattila, M.L. *et al.* (2010) Comorbid psychiatric disorders associated with Asperger syndrome/high-functioning autism: A community- and clinic-based study. *Journal of Autism and Developmental Disorders,* 40(9), 1080–1093.

Mazurek, M.O. & Sohl, K. (2016) Sleep and behavioral problems in children with autism spectrum disorder. *Journal of Autism and Developmental Disorders*, 46(6), 1906–1915.

McGillivray, J.A. & Evert, H.T. (2018) Exploring the effect of gender and age on stress and emotional distress in adults with autism spectrum disorder. *Focus on Autism and Other Developmental Disabilities*, 33(1), 55–64.

Nimmo-Smith, V. *et al.* (2020) Anxiety disorders in adults with autism spectrum disorder: A population-based study. *Journal of Autism and Developmental Disorders*, 50, 308–318.

Ommensen, B. (2023) A Life Lived in the Shadows: Social and Emotional Functioning in Older Autistic Adults and the Potential for Successful Ageing. PhD thesis, University of Queensland.

Porges, S.W. (2011) *The Polyvagal Theory: Neurophysiological Foundations of Emotions, Attachment, Communication, and Self-Regulation*. New York, NY: W.W. Norton & Co.

Sequeira, S. & Ahmed, M. (2012) Meditation as a potential therapy for autism: A review. *Autism Research and Treatment*, Article ID 835847.

Stewart, G. *et al.* (2020) Sleep problems and mental health difficulties in older adults who endorse high autistic traits. *Research in Autism Spectrum Disorders*, 77, 101633.

Van Steensel, F.J., Bögels, S.M. & Perrin, S. (2011) Anxiety disorders in children and adolescents with autistic spectrum disorders: A meta-analysis. *Clinical Child & Family Psychology Review*, 14(3), 302.

White, S.W., Oswald, D., Ollendick, T. & Scahill, L. (2009) Anxiety in children and adolescents with autism spectrum disorders. *Clinical Psychology Review*, 29(3), 216–229.

# Notes

....................................................
....................................................
....................................................
....................................................
....................................................
....................................................
....................................................
....................................................
....................................................
....................................................
....................................................
....................................................
....................................................
....................................................
....................................................
....................................................
....................................................